THE ILLUMINATED BOOKS
OF THE
MIDDLE AGES

THE
ILLUMINATED BOOKS
OF THE
MIDDLE AGES;

AN ACCOUNT OF THE DEVELOPMENT AND PROGRESS
OF THE ART OF ILLUMINATION,
AS A DISTINCT BRANCH OF PICTORIAL ORNAMENTATION,
FROM THE IVTH. TO THE XVIITH. CENTURIES.

BY

HENRY NOEL HUMPHREYS.

ILLUSTRATED BY

A SERIES OF EXAMPLES, OF THE SIZE OF THE ORIGINALS,
SELECTED FROM THE MOST BEAUTIFUL MSS. OF THE VARIOUS PERIODS,
EXECUTED ON STONE AND PRINTED IN COLOURS

BY

OWEN JONES.

BRACKEN BOOKS
LONDON

The Illuminated Books of the Middle Ages was originally published in 1849

This edition published in 1989 by Bracken Books,
an imprint of Studio Editions Ltd,
Princess House, 50 Eastcastle Street,
London W1N 7AP, England.

Copyright this edition © 1989 Studio Editions Ltd

Reprinted 1995

ISBN 1 85170 276 8

Printed and bound in Slovenia

CONTENTS

INTRODUCTION

REPRODUCTIONS OF ILLUMINATED MANUSCRIPTS are found everywhere – on Christmas cards, calendars, postcards, and as illustrations to books – by courtesy of modern photographic techniques which can give us facsimiles in full colour. We take this facility for granted today, though it is only a few decades old at most. But the attempt to reproduce by colour printing the full glories of the illuminated page goes back much further than this, further in fact than the Christmas card itself. The Victorian era harnessed new techniques of colour printing to the creation and satisfaction of a growing taste for the work of the scribe and illuminator in reproduction. The rapid development of chromo-lithographic techniques in the 1840s went hand in hand with a revival of interest in illumination, inspiring artists, designers, printers, and publishers to create new forms of books, calendars, and music covers, as well as a wealth of other kinds of printed ephemera.

Yet this aspect of the Gothic Revival tends to be forgotten today because other more visible productions in architecture, sculpture, metalwork, and panel paintings are still all around us, while the work of the illuminators and printers is buried in libraries. By the end of Victoria's reign, the mania for illumination as a source of ornament and design was waning, and the chromolithographic process was being challenged by new techniques of colour printing. The very success of photographic processes of reproduction has banished the techniques of the chromolithographers to oblivion, so that even amongst modern scholars of medieval illumination facsimiles are usually assumed to date from the beginnings of the four-colour halftone process. Photographic separations did not make colour reproduction better, but they certainly made it commercially more successful, because faster and cheaper. So both the Victorian revival of interest in illumination and the achievements of the chromolithographic process tend to be overlooked or underestimated.

But not by everybody. Dr A.N.L. Munby, Librarian of King's College, Cambridge, published *Connoisseurs and Medieval Miniatures 1750–1850* in 1972. This book is a landmark in the study of the taste for illumination as an aspect of the Gothic Revival. Munby pointed out that by 1850 medieval miniatures were no longer regarded as rude monkish drawings which reflected the barbarity of their age, but were seen as part of the history of European painting, from a period before panel paintings appeared in any great numbers. Most of Munby's book is devoted to the emergence of the new taste amongst bibliophiles, collectors, and scholars, but by 1850 he recognised that the chromolithographic facsimiles of illuminations were spreading this taste to a much wider audience. While the few, like Ruskin (who claimed that 'a well-illuminated missal is a fairy cathedral full of painted windows'), could indulge their taste by buying or borrowing medieval manuscripts and cutting out the miniatures for pasting into scrapbooks or making into collages, many more could demonstrate their enthusiasm less destructively by doing their own

1

illuminating after the reproductions newly published in gift-books and manuals. As Munby says, 'Illumination to medieval patterns vied with tatting and Berlin woodwork as a fitting pursuit for young ladies, and cheap methods of reproduction in colour, such as chromolithography, made illuminated manuscripts familiar to a much wider public' (p.1).

The Illuminated Books of the Middle Ages, which was first published complete in 1849 by Longman, was the best of the English chromolithographic books dedicated to the reproduction of pages from illuminated manuscripts, and has strong claims to being the finest specimen of chromolithographic printing of all sorts. It was not the first of such books in England, being preceded by *Palaeographia Sacra Pictoria* (1843–5), the work of J.O. Westwood, printed by William Smith (a new edition is published by Bracken Books, 1988). The idea for both works undoubtedly came from the publication in France of Count Bastard's enormous *Peintures des Manuscrits*, Paris, 1832–69, and Silvestre and Champollion's similarly monumental *Paléographie Universelle* (4 volumes, 301 plates), Paris, 1841. The English works were on a smaller scale, and did not rely on the use of hand-colouring to supplement chromolithography; thus they could be sold at a price which allowed many more people to buy them. *The Illuminated Books of the Middle Ages* sold at 21*s.*, like most of Humphreys' books, which, though not cheap, was certainly affordable by a middle-class book-buying public. In fact, as with other folio books of the period, *The Illuminated Books of the Middle Ages* appeared first in parts sold separately, which could be assembled by the owner and bound to his own orders (this accounts for the variable order of the plates as found in extant copies). Production of the plates extended over six years from 1844 to 1849, as printing each plate from a number of different stones inked in different colours, was an elaborate and time-consuming process.

A word is needed here about the chromolithographic process itself. Lithography of all sorts is a planographic process, that is to say the areas which print and those which do not are all on the same level (though strictly the chalk or crayon which draws on the stone is in minute relief on its surface). This distinguishes it from relief and intaglio processes, which had dominated the illustration of books up until the nineteenth century, and which involved the cutting out of a block to leave a raised surface in relief, or incising a surface so that ink might be retained once the surface was wiped. Lithography, which most often involved stone, but might also use zinc or other substances as a ground, developed as a faster and less mechanically tricky process of reproducing images in the nineteenth century. It was also much easier to make printing surfaces of stone than of copper or wood, which meant that plates could be much larger in size. As a process lithography relies on chemical principles, the antipathy of grease and water, and the attraction of these to their like and to a smooth porous ground (i.e. stone). The artist draws directly onto the stone with a chalk or crayon, with no need for an intermediary to transfer a design from a cartoon to a three-dimensional object. Right from the early days of lithography at the start of the century, experiments began to find ways of lithographic printing in colours, but really satisfactory methods of doing so did not come along until the 1840s, when printing in different colours from stones could be done in such a way that a wide range of different tints could be superimposed on one another. From this point onwards printers became very interested in the commercial possibilities of chromolithography, as it came to be called, and a new area of mass production of coloured images was under way.

The author and illustrator of *The Illuminated Books of the Middle Ages* was Henry Noel Humphreys, who was the most skilful exponent of the copying of illuminations in the new medium. Noel Humphreys was born in Birmingham on 4 January 1810, and little is known of his early life and career. We do know that he spent some years in Italy, where he interested himself in both natural history and art. He had evidently found opportunities to inspect illuminated manuscripts in the Vatican, the Ambrosiana Library in Milan, and other libraries, as his later writings and illustrations show. By 1840, however, he was back in England, and in that year, through Charles Tilt, he published *Rome, and Its Surrounding Scenery*. It contained illustrations by other 'eminent artists', though not by Humphreys himself, who provided only the text (the authority for this, and for much else on what is known of Humphreys and his work is Ruari McLean, *Victorian Book Design and Colour Printing*, 2nd edition, London, 1972, especially chapter 10, 'Henry Noel Humphreys, author and illustrator'). His next published work is the first to show an interest in medieval miniatures, *Illuminated Illustrations of Froissart*, published by William Smith in two volumes in 1844. The illustrations are lithographed, but hand-coloured, and do not bear comparison with his later work.

Humphreys must have been at work on the plates for *The Illuminated Books of the Middle Ages* from 1844 onwards, but this did not prevent his achieving an astonishing output of other productions between 1846 and 1849, to say nothing of the *Illuminated Calendars* for 1845 and 1846, published by Longman. These books include some of the most original pieces of book-making in the nineteenth or any other century. *The Coins of England*, written and illustrated by Noel Humphreys, includes woodcut initials in medieval style and twenty-four chromolithographic plates of coins printed in copper, silver, and gold against a royal blue background. Three books appeared in 1847 with Humphreys' own illustrations: *Parables of Our Lord*, *The Poets' Pleasaunce*, and *Insect Changes*. All of them show how Noel Humphreys was able to adapt the idiom of medieval illumination to purposes of modern edification and amusement. *Parables of Our Lord* consists of thirty-two pages of illumination through chromolithography, but these are not mere borrowings from medieval models, since, as Noel Humphreys says, he 'thought it more suitable that the garments of gold and many colours in which he has arrayed them [the ornamental borders], should at all events be *new*, rather than embroidery borrowed from old missals or other sources of conventional ornament, however quaint or beautiful'. The designs show how he put his knowledge of natural history to work, as well as expressing his admiration for Flemish fifteenth-century illumination.

The designs for *The Poets' Pleasaunce* include thirty full-page borders by Noel Humphreys, introducing each flower described by English poets, on this occasion all engraved in black and white. *Insect Changes* was written and illustrated by Noel Humphreys for children, with eight pages illuminated in ten- or twelve-colour chromolithography drawn in the style of the Book of Hours of Anne of Brittany (see Plate XXXI of this book). Each of these three books has a startling binding — for instance that of *Parables of Our Lord* is a 'papier-maché' binding, contrived to look like carved ebony. This was cast in a black plaster composition, over papier-maché, often reinforced with metal. As McLean points out, such an object could not be put on a shelf with other books; it could only rest on tasselled piano-covers. It is characteristic of many of Noel Humphreys books that their design is all-inclusive, though many of them have not survived in the pristine splendour of their original clothing. Noel Humphreys kept up this rate of production in 1848 (two illuminated books) and 1849 (no less than four!), including *The Art of Illumination and Missal Painting: A Guide to Modern Illuminators*. This last includes twelve chromolithographic reproductions of manuscripts, printed in up to as many as fourteen colours, with the same plates provided also in outline 'to be coloured by the Student according to the theories developed in the Work'. The binding is delightful, and one of the few surviving examples in good condition is in Cambridge University Library. It is in white leather, with a border blocked in gold on blue, and on the front a design printed in chromolithography on paper, inset and lined in gold.

On the last page of the book Noel Humphreys outlines the qualities required of an illuminator, quoted by Ruari McLean as an indication of the ideals by which he was guided in his own work:

> He must be acquainted with Botany, and also possess a knowledge of what may be termed the poetry of flowers, that is to say, their association, their symbolism, and their properties. Entomology, too, with its train of glittering flies, and painted caterpillars; those gorgeous worms, that in the tropics shine like creeping jewels, must have formed one of his pursuits. In short, Natural History in general, and the associations and emblematic character of various substances, plants, and animals, must form a portion of the education of an illuminator. He must thoroughly understand the laws of colours, and also their symbolism, and above all, he must possess a thorough knowledge of the history of decorative art in all ages . . .

The passage goes on to claim that he must also be familiar with poetry, early Christianity, and romance, as well as the lore of costume, weapons, and armour, the art of the old masters, and architecture, so that:

> the illuminator may lift his art to the high position which legitimately belongs to it; but which the poor productions of the last century and a half have tended so greatly to lower; reducing that which should be an exquisite art, to a routine of the most vulgar mechanism.

Apart from the lofty ambition, what is most striking to the modern eye in this passage is the alliance it proclaims between natural history and ornament, those most characteristic productions of high Victorian culture. Noel Humphreys distinguished penwork initials in illumination in very much the same spirit that he differentiated between species of beetle — and it was obvious to him that scientific classification in both areas depended on accurate illustration. Noel Humphreys' friend and rival J.O. Westwood, the author of *Paleographica Sacra Pictura*, shared the same ideals. He emphasised the interest in natural history above all else when he came to write Noel Humphreys' obituary in 1879, recalling their collaboration in a book on English butterflies and moths. But although Noel Humphreys continued after 1849 as a prolific author and illustrator, he was never able to make a great deal of money. When he died intestate after a sudden illness, at his house, 7 Westbourne Square in London, on 10 June 1879, letters of administration were granted to his son, Noel Algernon; he left under £800.

In his introduction to *The Illuminated Books of the Middle Ages*, Noel Humphreys makes it clear that his purpose in illustrating it is to show the development of illumination as a branch of ornament rather than of pictorial art. This is where he differs most from the earlier connoisseurs of medieval miniatures, who saw them primarily as examples of pictorial art before the rise of the panel painting. Noel Humphreys was more interested in matters like the symmetry of a page design, the development of partial and full borders, and the use of acanthus or ivy leaves as a basis for decoration, than in figurative style, or the subjects of miniatures. In showing the best examples of earlier style he hoped to influence modern design and counteract the sterile classicism which he felt had overtaken it since the mid seventeenth century:

4

The only style of general art in vogue was that founded on crude and meagre imitations of the worst classical models, producing, as practised, the most wretched effect on the art of other schools: for a French supremacy in art seems to have been acknowledged without dispute throughout Europe. This feeling of crudely copying antique art existed with more or less intensity till about 1820, when a reaction as extraordinary again took place; the works of the middle ages, and even the worst specimens of the worst periods, being sought with great avidity. This taste continued to extend, and within the last few years became a lamentable mania; the most servile imitations of the bad drawing, the crude combinations, and even the rude finishing, being considered evident marks of the most accomplished taste. A better feeling is now rising; the finest features of the art of any age are alone considered worthy of study or reproduction; and beautiful works of the middle ages are sought, not for the purpose of making close and servile copies of them with all their defects, but of studying the *principles* upon which they were composed, and with those principles producing works more in accordance with the spirit and sympathies of the present age, than the works of any former era can possibly afford.

Noel Humphreys' views on the development of illumination were very much conditioned by his interest in the principles of ornament and in classification. His introduction, and the notes accompanying each plate, distinguish between different styles which succeed each other from the fourth to the seventeenth centuries. He is dismissive of the paltry ornament of the Byzantines, and of their failure to develop over the course of centuries. On the other hand the intricate decoration of the early Irish and Anglo–Irish manuscripts – illustrated by the Lindisfarne Gospels – appeals to him as both original and capable of infinite variety. He is also an enthusiast for what he calls Opus Anglicum, the Anglo–Saxon style of the tenth century whose finest example is the Benedictional of St Ethelwold, but whose influence he finds at work in architecture and jewellery, and still sees potent as late as the fifteenth century in England. He is not very specific about the characteristics of this style, though remarking on the importance of architectural motifs and the use of gold. The twelfth-century style, flourishing all over Western Europe, he takes to be the apogee of illumination, 'the noblest style of illumination ever evolved during the whole thirteen centuries during which the art was practised'. This is what we would call today the Romanesque style, and Noel Humphreys typically characterises it not by its handling of the human figure but by the use of scrolled acanthus and the interweaving of the plant stems. In the fourteenth century he recognises the development of the framing of the page by bars decorated with foliage, what he calls 'the Gothic bracket', and the introduction of naturalistic rather than symbolic motifs. Except in Italy, European styles tend to develop away from symmetry towards the picturesque in the fifteenth-century, and Noel Humphreys obviously disapproves of the fragmentation and lack of coherence that this represents. He is willing to make obeisance towards the work of Giulio Clovio in the sixteenth century, as was customary among connoisseurs of the miniature in the nineteenth century, although this florid style is not described in more than perfunctory terms. In all, Noel Humphreys' sketch of the development of illumination in Europe is surprisingly recognisable, after all the work of modern scholarship, which has tended to underpin rather than undermine many of his judgments. His emphasis on the importance of ornamental features in distinguishing styles is entirely modern in its approach.

The list of manuscripts belonging to the different schools of decoration of illuminated manuscripts, which is arranged chronologically at the end of his introduction, is remarkably comprehensive for its time. Although Noel Humphreys confesses honestly enough at the end of the list that he has not actually inspected all the manuscripts, he is obviously aware of a much greater range of evidence for the history of illumination than most of his contemporaries. Most of the manuscripts in Noel Humphreys' list can still be located, despite difficulties with old-fashioned names and changed ownership, and would be recognised by any scholar as highlights in the development of medieval art. To put together a list of this size must have meant a good deal of searching on his part in both library catalogues and libraries themselves, at a time when many of the modern aids to such research were just not available. The owners of manuscripts in the list range from private individuals, most of them the great English collectors of the age – Robert Holford, Francis Douce, Sir Thomas Phillipps, etc. – to libraries in Vienna, Milan, Uppsala, Turin, Dublin, Paris, Rome, Stockholm, St Gall (Switzerland), Rouen, Munich, Bamberg, and Epernay, to say nothing of course of London, Oxford, and Cambridge. It is worth noting though that most of the later manuscripts are drawn from the British Museum or the Bodleian Library in Oxford, whereas the earlier ones are trawled from much further afield. The sheer numbers of fourteenth-, fifteenth-, and sixteenth-century examples scattered across Europe defied analysis then, as they still do today to a surprising degree.

The list of 39 plates illustrated in *The Illuminated Books of the Middle Ages* shows that Noel Humphreys copied mainly from manuscripts in the British Museum, the Bibliothèque Nationale and Bibliothèque de l'Arsenal in Paris, and the Soane Museum in London. His travels to Italy earlier in life no doubt gave him the opportunity to see many of the great treasures of the Vatican Library and the Ambrosiana in Milan in particular, but when it came to assembling plates for his book Humphreys was bound to fall back on those manuscripts he could consult most easily for copying purposes. He was evidently given permission to study the Benedictional of St Ethelwold then in the possession of the Duke of Devonshire, as well as manuscripts belonging to Robert Holford and his own collaborator Owen Jones. But it was the rich institutional collections in London and Paris which gave him sufficient range of materials to illustrate at least one example from each of the most significant schools of illumination, even those not native to England and France.

The plates of *The Illuminated Books of the Middle Ages* look very unlike the modern photographic facsimiles which we see reproduced in postcards, Christmas cards, and books. The glossy finish is missing of course, but what is most striking is the absence of the uniform tonal bias which is the mark of photographic techniques – no overall predominance of green or red to come between the viewer and the individual colours. On the other hand the chromolithographs tend to have a rather flat appearance, lacking the sense of depth given by the original work of the illuminators, where colour is often laid on at varying depths, and gold in particular stands off the page. The different colours available to the nineteenth-century colour printer as compared to the illuminator mean that there is no direct equivalence of colours between original illumination and chromolithograph. The printer had to choose which colours were to stand in for those used in Noel Humphreys' coloured copy of the original, and to try to balance them to achieve a comparable effect. Really these images should be looked at as reinterpretations of the original illuminations, whose aim is to highlight the ornamental impression of each leaf, rather than facsimiles which could hypothetically stand in for the original.

In this light the chromolithograph of the leaf from the Lindisfarne Gospels

(Plate I) is an extraordinary achievement by Noel Humphreys and his printer, Owen Jones. Noel Humphreys has tried to reproduce each individual feature of the incredibly complex pattern of the decoration, down to the tiny dots which are the constituent parts of the background decoration around the main letters. He has also copied the interlinear Anglo–Saxon glosses supplied by a later scribe in a cursive hand (though one such gloss to the left of the page has been omitted). At the minutest level there are a very few elements of draughtsmanship where Noel Humphreys has departed from the model of the original designer of the leaf, and then usually in the interest of his own decorative principles. In the 'P' of the 'INP' design there is an example in the feet of the letter (at more or less the very centre of the page). Noel Humphreys has used two circular patterns of acanthus in the feet of the 'P' where the original designer chose to use simple spiral patterns (as in the flourish below the bowl of the 'P', where Humphreys has copied it faithfully). This may well reflect Noel Humphreys' own preference for acanthus as a decorative motif, expressed in his admiration for the Romanesque style of illumination. But despite the differences in minutiae of pattern and in the colours used, Noel Humphreys has succeeded in recreating a design which is almost as striking an achievement as the original Lindisfarne illumination.

On close inspection of some of the other plates in comparison with the original illumination, it is possible to see some of Noel Humphreys' own decorative ideas taking over at the expense of simple copying. For instance the plate from the Benedictional of St Ethelwold (Plate VII) includes extra polychrome effects in the bases of the architectural columns, and the pattern of circles and rectangles below the feet of the confessors has been supplied by Noel Humphreys himself. To some extent this is a case of gilding the lily, though given the technical problems involved in creating the chromolithographs as copies of illuminations we might expect Noel Humphreys and his collaborators to sin in the other direction, by simply omitting details of decoration.

The plates are at their weakest in their handling of figures, and in particular of faces. As we have seen, Noel Humphreys was interested in ornament rather than figure painting, and he did not make the same effort to recreate the techniques of the originals in this area. In Plate IX, for example, the handling of the twisting tendrils of acanthus in the Arnstein Bible is assured, whereas no attempt has been made to render the characteristic strong lines of nose and eyebrow, the brown shadows and white highlights which model the faces. Instead, we have very bland and insipid faces, which look more like Victorian popular religious art than Romanesque painting. The same plate raises another problem area, that of the copying of script. Noel Humphreys has gone to considerable trouble to copy the individual strokes which make up each letter, but the overall impression lacks the rhythm of the original. The relationship of thick to thin strokes and the overall duct of the hand simply cannot be recreated in this way; and this is one area in which photographic techniques definitely score over chromolithography.

But these weaknesses should not prevent us delighting in the liveliness and variety to be found in the series of plates as a whole, encompassing as they do so many different styles of illumination and ornament. They would surely be an inspiration to any Victorian illuminator or bibliophile, as well as to any craftsman looking for appropriate and authentic medieval ornament for his modern design. As well as the series of plates there are also two pages of lithographic designs drawn from a range of manuscripts of different periods and styles, which an aspiring illuminator might try to colour by hand him or herself. One of the additional delights of the book is that Noel Humphreys has also treated some of the pages describing the plates as occasions for creating a unified design of type and chromolithographed ornament in the spirit of a medieval illuminator. He interprets the ornamental conventions of the period he is describing in an original design of his own. Thus the description of 'Les Merveilles du Monde' (Plate XV) has a bar at the left of the page, running over to a half bar at the top which is linked to a decorated initial 'A'. Both the bar and the initial are decorated in a style which borrows delightfully from fourteenth-century conventions without copying from any one manuscript.

The title page of *The Illuminated Books of the Middle Ages* tells us that Noel Humphreys' designs were 'executed on stone and printed in colours by Owen Jones'; and the contribution of the printer should not be forgotten. Owen Jones (1809–1874) began as an architect, but after a European tour which led him to sketch and paint the Alhambra, the Moorish palace at Granada, his attempts to get these lithographed led him to set up a printing establishment himself. Apart from the *Plans, Elevations, Sections and Details of the Alhambra* (1836), which was the first English chromolithographed work, Jones is best known today for his *Grammar of Ornament* (1856), but he specialised as a colour printer in the illuminated gift book, which made him a natural choice for Noel Humphreys. Strictly, however, it is not the case that all the plates were printed by Owen Jones. Some of them were 'printed in colours by C. Graf', whose business seems to have been smaller than that of Jones, though no less skilful. Plate XXIV, the 'Recollation of the Chronicles of England', written for Edward IV, was 'printed by Quinet's chromo-lithography', though it also bore the imprint of 'Day & Haghe, lithographers to the Queen'. Each of these plates, requiring different stones for every colour printed, would have been a complicated task in itself for the printer, and evidently over the six years in which they appeared Noel Humphreys decided to try printers other than Owen Jones, possibly because at times he was too busy. Jones's prominent position on the title page is a tribute paid to the skills of the chromolithographic printer.

Peter Murray Jones
FELLOW AND LIBRARIAN
KING'S COLLEGE, CAMBRIDGE

THE

ILLUMINATED BOOKS

OF THE

MIDDLE AGES.

THE OBJECT of the present sketch of the progress of the Art of Illumination, is not to treat the subject archæologically, but artistically, simply tracing the rise and progress of the art itself, without reference to the history of the books so decorated; or to any anecdotes or associations connected with them. It is not within the scope of the present plan either to dwell upon the biography, or even to refer to the few names which have been preserved of the artists who have enriched the art with their works; but simply to trace the rise and progress, through most of their remarkable phases, of the exquisite and distinct styles of *ornamentation* that have been gradually developed by the practice of enriching MSS. with illuminated *letters* and *borders*. To *miniatures*, belonging to a higher branch of the pictorial arts, I shall rarely allude, as the subject would carry me far beyond the limits of this work.

Some writers on the art of illumination appear to have considered that it arose at a period preceding the Christian era; others assign its origin to Rome, and consider that the later phases of declining Roman art were exhibited in its earliest productions; grafted upon which, the barbaric art which succeeded that of Rome, formed the earliest combinations of ornament, from which all the more modern styles of this class of art have successively arisen. This view, though true to a great extent, appears to me to require modification.

Allowing that the practice of illuminating MSS. may have commenced in Italy during the latter period of the Roman Empire, the utter extinction of its western division by the northern hordes, in the fifth century, allowed the art no time to develop itself ere the whole fabric of Roman civilization was swept away by the invading torrent of barbarism. We must therefore look to the Greek capital of the Eastern Empire; and I am inclined to believe that the custom of introducing gold and colours in the ornamentation of books, *originated* in the newly-founded city of Constantine. It is evident that the architects of Greece and Rome, when carried there to adorn that brilliant link of Europe and Asia with their works, soon became imbued with those peculiarities of style, flowing westward from the far East, which eventually grafted the pointed arch on the Roman column, and produced other combinations, which afterwards led to the various styles that have been termed Gothic, Lombardic, &c.; for it is quite certain that the arts of Constantinople, after the prostration of civilization in the West, exercised a wonderful influence over the disorganised European provinces of the shattered empire as they emerged from the confusion of the barbaric invasions. Another reason inducing me to believe that the art of illuminating MSS. *originated* there, is, that the earliest style of Byzantine ornament strongly resembles that found in the most ancient Persian MSS., and still more ancient sculptures. It also resembles in many particulars the sculptures recently discovered at Nimroud and Nineveh. But although the Byzantines, as I conjecture, borrowed the art from the East and established it in Europe, they never advanced beyond this first step. All their *decorations* were of an inferior character, producing an effect of somewhat barbaric oriental splendour, rather than one founded on true artistic principles or inventive design; and beyond this style they never advanced,—no material variation of style being evolved from the fourth to the fifteenth century. The same remark does not apply, however, to their miniatures, but I shall recur to these points farther on.

I must now attempt to sketch the short career of Roman book decoration, after which I shall briefly notice in greater detail the peculiarities of the Byzantine school, and then proceed to the successive styles of book illumination developed in Western Europe, which strictly form the subject of this work.

B

THE FOURTH AND FIFTH CENTURIES.—ROMAN AND BYZANTINE STYLES.

The Egyptians appear to have decorated their MSS. simply by the use of a vermilion colour for the characters at the commencement of leading passages; a practice no doubt followed in the MSS. of the Greeks, and also by the writers of MS. among the Romans, though the MSS. disinterred at Pompeii afford no traces of any decoration whatever. Pliny, however, states, that books in his time were decorated with pictures; and Dibdin has a laborious note on a passage in Pliny, referring to a collection of 700 notices by Varro of the eminent men of his time, illustrated by portraits. This book, or a copy of it, appears to have been seen by Symmachus at the end of the fourth century, who speaks of it in one of his letters.

The earliest Latin MSS. that present any traces of pictorial decoration, do not date earlier than the fourth century, and in these cases there is little in the ornament of a good decorative character. The Roman Calendar of the Vienna Library, supposed to have been executed about 354, during the reign of Constantine the Younger, for a certain Valentinus, is perhaps the earliest and most interesting specimen. The Vatican Virgil has but little ornament; its illuminations,* or rather illustrations, being composed of figures shaded in bistre, apparently with a pen; whilst the great Virgil of St. Denis, formerly at the Vatican, has the outlines filled up rudely with heavy colours. Of enriched initials, or ornamental borders, worthy of notice, these early Latin MSS. have none; at least no MSS. so ornamented have come down to us. It is, therefore, to early Byzantine MSS. that we must look for the first glittering traces of illumination in its true meaning. In the fifth century, they begin to exhibit small borders on gold grounds, surrounding the miniature pictures. The MS. Dioscorides at Vienna, executed by order of the Empress Juliana Anicia, in the year 505, has some borders of a somewhat higher character,† but our accompanying outline plate, from Agincourt's great work, will give a good general idea of the meagre style of border in general use. Soon after, an ornamental heading to the principal pages was adopted in the same school, of the style of which the outline, No. 2, from the Codex Ebnerianus, at Oxford, is a good example, though belonging to a later period. The Byzantine artists, though not excelling in ornament, long preserved in their miniature pictures a reminiscence of the artistic feeling of their Greek ancestors, and their early treatment of various Christian subjects became types long followed by Western artists; who were, however, more independent in their style of *ornaments*. The peculiar mode of ornamentation of the Eusebian Canons, in Latin MSS., which accompanied nearly all copies of the Gospels, from the fifth or sixth, to the thirteenth century, was, however, probably founded on Byzantine originals, as a very early Greek example exists of the columnar separation surmounted by arches, in the same manner as is shown in our plate from the Golden Gospels. The accompanying outline (No. 2 ½) is from the finest example known, being a manuscript which may possibly be of a date as early as the fourth or fifth century. It is written, and the ornaments are likewise painted, on a gold ground. It is preserved in the British Museum, and

numbered "Additional, 5111." The patterns are fine samples of this peculiar style, of which, however, there are no instances of any florid varieties. This fragment should be carefully compared with the plate from the Eusebian Canons of the Golden Gospels, as the comparison will show how far the Western illuminators borrowed from Byzantine models.

The Western illuminators, though following the general distribution of eastern decoration, did not imitate its details, which in their hands became wonderfully intricate and various.‡

Another peculiarity found in some early MSS., which perhaps owes its origin to Byzantine calligraphers, is the custom occasionally adopted, of staining the vellum purple, and executing the writing in silver or gold; a few MSS., all prior to the tenth century, still exist so written—the majority Greek.

The magnificent Pentateuch, on purple vellum, written in letters of silver and gold, at Vienna, is perhaps the most magnificent specimen of this style of writing; specimens of which, Lambecius has engraved in a series of plates. But the celebrated Codex purpureo-argenteus, written about A.D. 360, which has found its way to Upsal, in Sweden, where it is still preserved, is the most ancient example of a *MS.* on purple vellum, and perhaps the most ancient known illuminated MS. of any description, for its date is pretty well ascertained. Ulphilas appears to have translated the Gospels into Gothic, for the use of the Goths who settled among the Roman colonies of Wallachia in the fourth century; and it is therefore allowed at present, on the evidence collected by Knittel and Ihre, to take precedence over every other MS. of this character. It contains the greater part of the New Testament in a nearly perfect state.

Latin examples of MSS. on purple vellum of later period are more numerous than Greek. The Prayer-book of Charlemagne, in the library of the Louvre, and that of his grandson, Charles the Bald, in the Bibliothèque Nationale, are sufficient to show that the practice was continued as late as the ninth century; and there are examples to prove that after the art of staining the vellum was lost, it was imitated by *painting* one side of the vellum purple.

As the Byzantine styles did not either progress themselves, nor materially influence the progress of the beautiful styles of illumination that arose in the West of Europe, beyond the particulars above mentioned, I shall dismiss the former with this short notice; only recurring to the subject once to notice a Greek work of the fifteenth century, illustrated in this work, for the purpose of showing how little the main features of the style had varied in a thousand years. In concluding my remarks on the Byzantine school of illumination, I may add that the ornamental cappings or head-pieces above alluded to, sometimes contained a miniature, and that the initial letters were occasionally composed of figures fantastically arranged, like the accompanying outline of a T (our outline, No. 3), from Dibdin's "Decameron," taken from a Greek MS. formerly in the possession of J. Dent, Esq. But the feeling was generally meagre, as in the adjoining

---

* The term "illumination" appears to be of earlier origin than the thirteenth century, as it occurs in the well-known passage of Dante—

"——— quel arte,
Che alluminar é chiamata in Parisi."

† Engraved by Biscioni.

‡ Another legacy of Byzantine calligraphy may be cited, which is the abbreviated form of the words Jesus and Christus, for which the *Greek* characters were long preserved, and even now the monogram or abbreviation of the former is still so written— IH͞Σ being composed of the Greek I (iota), the long Greek e, H (eta), and the Greek final s, Σ (sigma); the omission of the 'su' being shown by the usual bar or mark of abbreviation, which was however omitted as its meaning became lost. The Byzantine monogram or abbreviation of Christus was XPΣ; the Greek ch, X (chi), the Greek r, P (rho), and the Greek final s, Σ (sigma); the 'istu' being omitted, and the omission indicated by the usual mark of abbreviation. In Western MSS. the Σ soon became s, and the H h, with the bar or mark of abbreviation, extended through the first stroke of the h, in order to form a representation of the crucifix.

outline E (No. 4), from the Codex Ebnerianus.* But though the details of the style are always meagre, they are sometimes, in the headings, &c., spread over a considerable space, and with their glittering gold ornaments have a rich appearance, approaching the more modern Persian illuminations which are founded upon similar principles of art—namely, the extension of the same small and generally simple pattern, longitudinally, to form a border; or repeated over a continued surface to form a mass of ornament, producing an effect similar to that of the ever-recurring patterns of a modern carpet. The same may be said of the ancient Syriac and Armenian illuminations, which are but variations of common Byzantine art. The annexed portion of a border from a Greek MS. of the eleventh century, from an example given in Dibdin "Decameron" (outline, No. 5), will exemplify the style of design alluded to.

It was in the West that the extraordinary variety and fertility of invention that distinguishes the art of the illuminator arose, and its earliest essays at invention in that part of Europe, appearing as they did, in conjunction with a rising instead of a sinking form of civilization, became allied to its progressive principles, and instinct with its fresh vitality. The most debased forms of Roman art formed the rude style first exhibited in early Gallican MSS., but nothing of that era was produced worthy of illustration in this work, as a distinct style; the purpose of this short treatise being, not the discussion of archæological rarities, but an examination of the most marked and superior styles evolved in the progress of the art. I may here, however, mention that, of a debased form of Roman art, the Latin Gospels of St. Augustine, now in Corpus Christi College, Cambridge, of the fifth or sixth century, are a very remarkable and authentic monument.†

For references to MSS. of Greek and Roman character of the fourth, fifth, and sixth centuries, see the appended list.

THE SIXTH, SEVENTH, AND EIGHTH CENTURIES.—IRISH AND ANGLO-IRISH STYLES.

Example.—A PAGE FROM THE GOSPELS OF LINDISFARNE, COMMONLY KNOWN AS THE "DURHAM BOOK," B. M. COT. NERO. D. IV.

The first style illustrated in this work by a fac-simile of an entire page, is that truly remarkable one that appears to have arisen in Ireland ‡ about the sixth or seventh century. The Book of Kells, preserved in Trinity College, Dublin, is perhaps the finest monument of the style in existence. The page from the Lindisfarne Gospels, commonly known as the Durham Book, from which our first plate is taken, exhibits its general features equally well. The style is formed by the most artistic and ingenious disposition of interweaving threads, bands, or ribbons of various colours, upon black or coloured grounds, varied by the introduction of extremely attenuated lizard-like reptiles, birds, and other animals, similarly treated. The initial letters are of enormous size, and of extreme intri-

* Now in the Bodleian Library, Oxford.

† Described by Mr. Westwood in the Palæogr. Sacra Pict., and by the Rev. Mr. Goodman in the 13th number of the Publications of the Cambridge Antiquarian Society.

‡ Lombardic MSS. have some affinities to this remarkable style, and works of a similar character are said to have been executed in the North and West of France about the same period, but the Irish are by much the finest examples.

cacy; the altered form of the fine Roman character being the basis or framework of the design of these letters. Such letters, and also the borderings, are generally surrounded with one or more rows of minute red dots; and another peculiarity is, that the *whole* of the writing on the principal pages is generally kept large, and made decorative, either by a coloured ground, or the introduction of masses of colour within, or between the letters. By referring to the plate, it will be seen that it is a very striking and remarkable style, and perfectly free from any admixture of Roman art, neither the acanthus leaf, nor any other feature of Roman ornament, forming any portion of the composition; the *forms* of the letters alone being based upon those of the Roman character, while all their details of ornament are original.

It is a style capable of great variety of treatment without departing from its general principles, of which I have said more in my description of the illustrative plate. It continued in practice without admixture in part of Wales and Ireland as late as the twelfth century, but on the Continent it became mingled with what has been termed the Charlemagne style, to be spoken of hereafter; and in England, in conjunction with rude Anglo-Saxon art, a style was formed that may be termed Anglo-Hibernian; but which latter, as inferior to the pure style, I shall not dwell upon.

For references to MSS. in Irish and Anglo-Irish style, see the appended list.

THE EIGHTH AND NINTH CENTURIES.—THE ANGLO-SAXON AND CHARLEMAGNE OR CAROLINE STYLES.

Examples.—THREE PAGES FROM THE GOLDEN GOSPELS, B. M. HARL., 2788; TWO PAGES FROM THE ATHELSTAN CORONATION BOOK, B. M. COT. TIBERIUS, A. 2; AND A PAGE FROM A BIBLE EXECUTED FOR CHARLES THE BALD, B. M. HARL., 7551.

About the period of Alfred the Great, in England, and Charlemagne on the Continent, considerable intercourse began to take place with Italy, and an admiration for the last remnants of Roman art still remaining in her provinces, which in Gaul were very numerous, led to their being sought as models. The result of this study, was a great simplification in the styles of illumination; and a debased form of the Roman acanthus began to be employed both in sculptural and pictorial decoration. The most perfect and consistent development of the new style, was perhaps that called the Charlemagne style, in which the feature of interlacing bands and animals was almost entirely abandoned, and the partial bordering more sparingly used. A fair example of this style is the (so-called) Alcuin Bible in the British Museum; but a much finer treatment of it is exhibited in a Psalter of Charles the Bald, preserved in the Bibliothèque Nationale of France. In the corresponding Anglo-Saxon period, a much stronger admixture of the interlaced work appeared; the great initials being formed, like those of the Continental style, by gold or silver bands; but much more intricately interlaced at the extremities. Our examples from the Gospels of Athelstan, the grandson of Alfred (though considered by some to have been executed on the Continent), exhibit in the initial I the peculiarities described. But the grandest style formed by the junction of the Anglo-Irish style with one founded on debased Roman.

is that exhibited in the Golden Gospels, from which we have given three superb examples.

This may be called a distinct style, as the interlacing features, with their dark rich colouring, are so happily blended with the grand and simple Roman forms as to make the union most effective: whilst a leading feature of Irish origin, that of making the whole of the writing of the principal pages decorative, has been preserved with striking effect, as shown in our second specimen from this fine MS. This latter is a feature that disappears in later specimens both of English and Continental art of this era, at all events in the very complete and well-knit form exhibited in the specimen alluded to. But some Continental MSS. of the ninth and tenth centuries exhibit the Charlemagne, or, as it may be termed, Franco-Roman* style, allied to the interlacing features of the Irish and Anglo-Irish styles, in which the peculiar characteristics of the latter predominate. Such is the feeling exhibited in a Bible illuminated for Charles the Bald, the grandson of Charlemagne, from which our next specimen is taken. This is very interesting, as showing the strong vital principles of a strictly new and original style (I allude to the pure Irish work of the sixth century), for not only do we find it existing unmixed at home for the long period of six centuries — specimens being in existence executed as late as the year 1200 A.D. — but we here find its leading features carried by the early Anglo-Saxon and Irish Missionaries to the Continent, and not only influencing, but actually predominating in many works of the well-established style of the Charlemagne period. Such is the case in our specimen from the Bible of Charles the Bald. The Charlemagne style and its varieties may be said to have prevailed on the Continent from the eighth to the tenth century, and was principally practised at Aix la Chapelle and the surrounding regions.

In some instances, the name of the calligrapher is appended to early MSS., and it would possess a certain artistic interest if it could be verified that this personage was also the illuminator; but this is a disputed point among archæologists, by whom these ancient names are perhaps unjustly shorn of their repute and station in the illustrious line of early artists. I am myself inclined to consider the writer and illuminator as one personage up to the twelfth or thirteenth centuries, after which the writing of books became a species of manufacture, and it is well known that the office of writer and illuminator were perfectly distinct; and in some cases the division of labour was carried much farther — different artists being employed on different styles of work in the same volume.

For references to MSS. of the Charlemagne period, see the appended list.

TENTH AND ELEVENTH CENTURIES. — THE STYLE SUPPOSED TO BE THE "OPUS ANGLICUM" MENTIONED BY AUTHORS OF THE PERIOD.

Examples.—A PAGE FROM THE BENEDICTIONAL IN THE POSSESSION OF THE DUKE OF DEVONSHIRE, AND ONE FROM A PSALTER IN THE BRITISH MUSEUM, ROYAL I. D. IX.

Styles similar to the Charlemagne style and its allied modi-

---

* The earliest French MS. may be termed Gallican in style, as exhibiting the latest Roman art as modified by its practitioners in that province. The Franks mingled a barbaric style with it, forming what may be termed a Franco-Gallican style, while the last phase shows the abandoning of the Gallican features for a Franco-Roman combination.

---

fications continued to prevail during this period, but the miniature pictures became much more numerous and elaborate, numbers being executed only in outline, but with much spirit, forming very interesting records of the arms, dresses, and manners of the period; but these do not belong to the strictly decorative features of book ornamentation which form the object of the present work.

About the tenth century, a distinct style appeared in England, which, without displacing others, was practised to a great extent for about two centuries. The specimens we have given from the Duke of Devonshire's Benedictional, and from a MS. in the British Museum, will be sufficient to show the characteristics of this rich and magnificent style, which we have every reason to consider national; no specimens existing in libraries of the Continent, except such as are known to have come originally from England, as is the case with the two splendid MSS. at Rouen.

This style, with its artistically arranged bars of gold, forming complete broad and noble frames to the text, and with which foliage is made to interlace with such an original effect, though it disappears after the eleventh century in the completeness of its original character, yet formed the basis of later styles which are nearly as national. For instance, in our specimen page from the Salisbury Lectionarium, a work of the end of the fourteenth century, the two gold bars will be observed forming massive corners, and enriched with interweaving foliage upon a similar *principle*, though of course very different in the detail, which exhibits the peculiar feeling of the later period—namely, less positive symmetry of corresponding parts, more general variety and slenderness of form, and generally a greater angularity of treatment; while figures, architectural features, and other objects are introduced with great profusion. Still, the *principles* of the grand tenth century style will be found to form its basis. The same may be said of the style which succeeded that of the Salisbury Lectionarium early in the fifteenth century, as will be seen on reference to our examples of that period from Mr. Owen Jones' Psalter, and the page from the poems of Lydgate. The magnificent style of the tenth century, which I believe to be the Opus Anglicum, held in such estimation on the Continent at that period, is therefore not only admirable in itself, on account of its completeness and very distinct character, but also as forming the basis of two later, and both, *national* styles. Most of the grand MSS. in the peculiar style of the tenth century, appear to have been executed at Winchester, where, it would seem, an especial school of illumination was founded under the patronage of the great Bishop Ethelwold.

For references to MSS. in this style, see the appended list.

ILLUMINATIONS OF THE TWELFTH CENTURY.

Example.—A PAGE FROM THE ARNSTEIN BIBLE, B. M. HARL., 2798 & 2799.

A new and more florid style of initial letters arose about the eleventh century, formed principally of interlacing branches, sometimes terminating in the heads of animals, and at other times interwoven with animals, the spaces between the ornaments generally filled alternately with light blue and delicate green. This style continued to acquire richness and distinctness until it resolved itself in the twelfth century into a very remarkable and highly decorative style; perhaps the noblest style of illumination ever evolved during the whole thirteen centuries during which the art was practised. It is principally founded upon the scrolling acanthus, as exhibited in the most florid Roman friezes, but rendered infinitely more intricate, and the details treated in the crisp and peculiar manner of the period—the circling *stems* forming a more prominent part in the composition than the *foliage*, whilst in the Roman frieze-work the foliage is principal and the stems completely subordinate. The fine style of the twelfth century flourished all over Western Europe, but appears to have been practised with most success in Rhenish Germany. It exhibited itself not only in the art of illumination but also in sculpture, in stained glass, and in gold and silver work, in each modified by the nature of the material.

In illuminated books this style is seldom found so highly enriched with colour, or forming such large compartments as in our specimen; more generally it is confined to large initial letters, some of which are coloured, but very rarely enriched with gold, being more generally only outlined in red with exquisite precision and effect, and frequently most elaborate in their composition. Even when only outlined in red they have occasionally a background coloured differently in the different compartments, and the effect so produced is, I believe, the foundation of the well-known Italian style, formed of white interlacing branches on variously-coloured grounds, that arose about the middle of the fifteenth century.

It is to be regretted that the fine style of the twelfth century is never, in illumination, found applied to *borders;* for it is evident that if its artists had given it that direction, it is capable of lending itself with the greatest and most beautiful effect to that form of book decoration.

Illuminations being almost the only examples of pictorial ornament of the early periods that have come down to us, are consequently very important records, enabling the architect to restore the decayed polychromic effect of some of our finest monuments in their true characters. This has been accomplished with the happiest effect in the restoration of the Temple Church, great part of which is work of the twelfth century, and the florid ornaments of illuminated books of the period have furnished the style of the newly painted decorations.

The fine style of the twelfth century may be divided into two distinct schools. In the one, the interweaving branches remain white, the grounds alone being coloured. In the other, the interweaving branches themselves are richly coloured, and the ground is gold, or of some deeper tone of colour. In the style that arose in Italy in the fifteenth century, founded upon the Northern styles of the twelfth, as above suggested, the same distinct phases of treatment may be observed, the earlier specimens being composed of branch-work left white, of which the effect may be seen in our page from a MS. Juvenal; whilst, in a later and rarer style, the branch-work is highly coloured, as in our splendid example from the MS. of Aulus Gellius.

I have above suggested that the styles of the twelfth century might have formed exquisite *borders*, whereas they are generally confined to the composition of initial letters. The Italian styles, just alluded to, and to be referred to hereafter, are, however, beautiful illustrations of the exquisite adaptation of the twelfth century styles to that feature of illumination.

I cannot close this brief account of the styles of illumination which prevailed in the twelfth century, without alluding to a singular variety presented in the fine MS. now forming part of the Egerton collection in the British Museum, (No. 1139.) The exquisitely carved ivory cover of this MS. is evidently its original binding, and is a most beautiful monument of the art of carving at the period. The MS. itself appears to have been executed at Constantinople, but by a western caligrapher and illuminator. The peculiarity of the style of the beautiful initial letters consists in their being entirely gold richly shaded with black, of which I know no other example. The volume also contains many miniatures, evidently by a Byzantine artist of the period, which possess no particular interest except that arising from their very beautiful state of preservation.

For references to MSS. of the twelfth century, see the appended list.

THE THIRTEENTH CENTURY.

Examples.—A PSALTER IN THE BRITISH MUSEUM, LANSDOWNE 431; THE HOURS OF ST. LOUIS; AND A PSALTER IN THE POSSESSION OF H. HOLFORD, ESQ.

The first style to be noticed in the thirteenth century is one which is evidently a highly-wrought working out of that of the twelfth; the same scrolling and interscrolling is rendered much more intricate and more slender, and the details more accurately finished and more various; a profusion of figures both of the human subject and animals being introduced, generally in illustration of the text, but occasionally in an arbitrary manner and with the sole view of decorative effect. Large square compartments, occupying an entire page, or a large portion of it, which are of rare occurrence in the twelfth century, become common in the thirteenth, and are generally surrounded by small mouldings, or rather borderings, of very delicate design and execution; such is the style exemplified by our specimen from a magnificent Psalter of the period, in the British Museum.

In the style treated of in the twelfth century, and in this style of the thirteenth century, miniature pictures are of rare occurrence; the decorative features being, at all events, completely predominant. But a style arose on the Continent of a nearly opposite character, of which our specimen from the *Hours* of St. Louis forms a good example, in which the miniatures became principal, and the borders which surround them entirely subordinate, forming merely a simple frame to the picture; the large initials also being made to form frames to miniatures—the whole letter also inclosed in a square frame formed of narrow borderings similar to those of the miniatures. These borderings are evidently founded upon the style of illumination peculiar to early Byzantine MSS., but they appear to have been modified by a more modern Italian feeling—the *oriental* character of detail having nearly disappeared. It is probable that this style of ornament, based upon Byzantine models but much modified, arose in Italy, from which it spread to France during the active intercourse caused by the crusade of St. Louis.* It was not, however, the style in most general practice; that of the *Psalter* of St. Louis,† which presents the usual characteristics described of the twelfth and thirteenth centuries, being much more common. It was my original intention to have given a specimen from that fine

* Some MSS. of this period are profusely filled with miniatures inclosed in neat borderings founded upon small Byzantine patterns; such, for instance, is the Bestiarium of the Ashmolean Museum at Oxford;—a curious work on the nature of beasts, of which several copies—more or less beautifully illuminated—are known to exist.

† The Psalter of Louis, or rather of Queen Blachne, preserved in the Library of the Arsenal, Paris.

c

MS., but my space has not allowed me to do so.* The next style to be noted in this century is that in which, while much of the peculiar detail and *circular* feeling of the early part of the century is preserved, the *angular* and peculiarly Gothic sentiment began to prevail, though in a manner scarcely definable; but which was to appear in the beginning of the next century in a pure and distinct form. Of this style the Psalter in the collection of Mr. Holford is a good specimen. The latest features of the styles of the thirteenth century were the introduction of the long-tailed initials, which formed a sort of border to one side of the page, terminating in a scroll, or curved leaf, at the bottom, and sometimes passing beneath the lower portion of the text. Of this style I have not space for a specimen; but as the style was not highly decorative nor complete in itself, but only forming a link to that well-marked style which was developed early in the next century, the omission is less to be regretted. In some cases the tailed letter was formed into a dragon, which bordered with a narrow ground of gold formed an almost regular border, upon which some of the illuminations of the fifteenth century were eventually founded.

The most exquisite illuminations of the thirteenth century, in which miniatures formed a leading feature, were undoubtedly executed in Paris, where a school of illumination was formed about this time which evidently took the lead of all others, and acquired that celebrity which led Dante to mention the art as one exclusively Parisian. Some of the French works of this period display an elegance in the drawing of the human figure, and drapery, almost amounting to affectation. A magnificent example of French art of this period (about 1300) has been recently acquired by the Museum (Add. 17,341), in which the miniatures, aided by the usual scroll-work, exquisitely treated, are made to form marginal bars, or exterior borders, which are profusely introduced and wonderfully elaborated. A common device of this epoch, for the first page of the Bible was one, formed of seven medallions, containing the story of the creation. A MS. Bible of the thirteenth century, in the Soane Museum, contains a beautiful border of this character.†

For references to MSS. of the thirteenth century, see the appended list.

THE FOURTEENTH CENTURY.

Examples.—THE PRAYER-BOOK OF THE DUKE OF ANJOU BIB. NAT. PARIS; THE SALISBURY LECTIONARIUM, B. M., HARL. 7028; THE COLLECTION OF TRAVELS ENTITLED "THE WONDERS OF THE WORLD," BIB. NAT. FOND, FRAN. 8392; AND THE BIBLE OF POPE CLEMENT VII., BIB. NAT. COLBERT, 18.

Every style of art branches eventually into many ramifications and subordinate styles of similar character before a new and pure style is finally evolved from its gradually separating and decomposing atoms.‡ It would carry me far beyond the limits of this work to attempt to define every variety produced by the expansion of the latter styles of the thirteenth century; I must therefore confine myself to stating that early in the

fourteenth century, the irregular bar or border formed by the foliaged or dragon-formed tail of some principal initial letter, gave way to a complete *bracket* formed of a variously-coloured bar, terminating at top and bottom in a clip or branch formed of ivy leaves, the angular and crisp character of which gave the highest *Gothic* character yet developed by the art of illumination, and completed a feeling of *pictorial* decorative art felicitously in harmony with the decorative sculpture of the great architectural works of the day. The bracket inclosing the description of the page from " Les Merveilles du Monde" is a fair example of the style.

A pleasing cotemporary style was an enriched variation of the ivy branch bracket, which arose in the reign of Edward III., having also for its principal feature the ivy branch, the leaves and stalks of which are coloured alternately blue and red, relieved with white, with which figures and mottos were interwoven with great boldness and some skill. The illuminated marginal band to the grant investing the Black Prince with the principality of Aquitaine, will convey an idea of the style; it is preserved among the records at Westminster. The Cotton MS. Nero VI., contains a copy of the treaty of Bretigny, to which is attached a miniature of King John of France, inclosed in ornamentation of a similar character. This style had been gradually led up to since about the time of Edward I., when the long-tailed letters, as mentioned at page 5, began to be formed into complete frames or borders to the page, gradually introducing ivy leaves and other floral features. A very fine specimen of that period is the Psalter once in the possession of Mr. Douce, and now deposited in the Bodleian Library. Our outline specimen, No. 5½, is from the last-named MS., and exhibits the features alluded to. It forms an angle of the irregular border or framework to one of the principal pages.

The period of the introduction of the well-defined Gothic bracket, was that of William of Wickham and his cotemporaries; when Gothic architecture, after progressing triumphantly through several remarkable phases, at length arrived at a distinct development, as well defined and as complete and homogeneous in all its parts as the purest styles of the architecture of Greece or Rome, of which, in its complete distinctness, it formed the very antipodes, and yet was equally beautiful, in a perfectly fresh and novel beauty; and perhaps in principles of structure, more scientific. It was a great artistic era—the architecture, the painting, the goldsmith's work, the elaborate productions in enamel, and the illuminator's art, were all in beautiful harmony; being each founded upon similar principles of design and composition:—even the art of writing lending itself to complete the grand chord of artistic harmony, by adopting that crisp and angular feeling which the then general adoption of the pointed arch introduced into all works of artistic combination. The bracket, or variously-coloured bar, of the illuminator, soon began to develop itself in richness and floridness of character: though at first somewhat meagre, towards the middle of the century it had become highly decorative, by greater intricacy in the branching of the ivy leaves, and by the introduction of birds and other objects, sometimes singular grotesques, among the ivy foliage. Of this fine development of the style, before any of its purity had lost itself in the unsuitable and extraneous details afterwards grafted

---

* One of its pages is, however, figured in Mr. Westwood's Illuminated Illustrations of the Bible, and exhibits another peculiarity of the style, namely, the scrolls or branches terminating in elaborate flower-like ornaments.
† Figured in my " Art of Illumination and Missal Painting."
‡ The last features of the richer and more intricate styles of the thirteenth century, especially that which branched out into the long-tailed initials, ex-

tended itself into complete borders in the beginning of the fourteenth century, forming a very remarkable style, of which I much regret that I have not room for a specimen. But I refer the student to the splendid MS. in the British Museum—Arundel 83; the beautiful Psalter in the possession of Lord Braybrook; and an exquisite MSS. in the Burgundian Library at Brussels, all three pure specimens of the style.

upon it, the page from the Prayer-book of the Duke of Anjou is a remarkably fine example. It exhibits all the richness, angular treatment, and generally elaborate character of the finest cotemporary monuments of sculpture and architecture.

It is here to be remarked that about the time of the introduction of the *Gothic bracket*, miniatures illustrative of the subject began to be profusely interpolated in the text; and other works than the Sacred Scriptures (in former periods nearly the only subjects deemed worthy of the intricate labours of the illuminator) began to be multiplied by calligraphers and illuminators. The songs of the troubadours and trouveres, and metrical and prose romances, were now about to find a public greedy of their wonders, and their poetry; and this circumstance tended greatly to modify the style of treating miniature pictures, and caused them to descend gradually from the emblematic or symbolic style in which sacred subjects had been treated, to the more natural manner in which it was found attractive to illustrate popular poems and legends. These miniatures were at first painted on a solid gold ground, after the manner of the ancient Byzantine works, the Oriental but somewhat barbaric splendour of which in this particular was long copied in the West. But the Western illuminators, who had long emancipated themselves from the formalities of Byzantine ornament, now abandoned the old gold ground of their miniature pictures; first adopting instead, delicate Mosaic patterns formed of small squares of gold and colours infinitely varied, of which I should have much wished to give a specimen, had the limits of this book permitted it. The next background was formed of intricate scroll-work, generally of two or three tones of the same colour, most frequently blue or red; then came a damasked pattern of gold upon a richly-coloured ground, and eventually, a natural background formed by a landscape or architectural interior. But this last change did not generally take place till quite the end of the fourteenth, or beginning of the fifteenth century; and even then, miniatures with *Mosaic* or *scroll* backgrounds are frequently found in the same volume alternately with others having a well-executed *natural* background, as late as the middle of the fifteenth century. Our specimen from the Prayer-book of the Duke of Anjou exhibits the miniature with the scrolled background in two colours, and is a specimen of the very highest class of that phase of art, the drawing and character of the figures being really very fine and expressive, and the damask scrolling of the background exquisitely designed and elaborated — the high finish of which is but imperfectly represented by our copy, the original being executed with the greatest conceivable degree of careful pencilling.

During the prevalence of this and other allied styles throughout the latter portion of the fourteenth century, very brilliant colours were sought by the illuminators, and the scarlet and blue then in use, especially the former, have never since been equalled.

This is the place to speak of three other very distinct styles which were practised during the fourteenth century. Our fac-simile of a page from the magnificent Salisbury Lectionarium, is the first I shall allude to. It will be seen, on reference to my remarks on the peculiar English style of the tenth century, that the principles of ornament then employed — foliage interweaving with gold bars — was now renewed in a more florid and varied manner. I there alluded to the style of the Salisbury Lectionarium now under notice, which is evidently founded on the leading features of the earlier period, and is also a style peculiarly English, being rarely if ever found in Continental MSS. of the

time. I need not farther refer to its details, as they are fully discussed in the description of the specimen, except by mentioning that the ivy-leaf *bracket* before referred to is sometimes treated in a manner that forms a link between this style and that of the tenth century.

The next style to be distinguished is that of our specimen from the fine MS. in the French Library, entitled "Les Merveilles du Monde," exhibiting a very peculiar treatment of foliage of arbitrary colours, enriched by a partial gold ground. This is a remarkable style, of which I know but two other specimens, both MSS. in the British Museum (Egerton, 1070, and Harl., 4947), the last of which may have been executed by the same hand. It would be difficult to name any other style with which it has a close analogy—most of its detached features may be found in the works of the following century, but nowhere, except in the MSS. mentioned, have I found them forming general compositions in the same peculiar feeling. The other *principal* pages in "Les Merveilles du Monde" have borders of the same character, but very various both in detail and general effect, showing that it is a style capable of wonderful development. The ordinary pages of "Les Merveilles du Monde" have the common ivy-leaf bracket of the period.

The last style of the fourteenth century which I shall dwell upon, is the very peculiar and elegant one which was developed in Italy at this period. It appears, like the Gothic bracket of English and French illuminators, to have originated in the long-tailed initials of the preceding century, which became at length in both instances a marginal bar or bracket. But in Italy the angular *Gothic* feeling never predominated as in the countries north of the Alps; the sharp ivy leaf never became a favourite feature in their illuminations; and we find instead, in their graceful and peculiar illuminations of the fourteenth century, a reminiscence of the acanthus treated in a peculiar manner, evidently founded on the Byzantine style of treating foliaged ornaments. The general composition is, however, quite distinct from Byzantine feeling. In the miniatures it is true there is a strong tincture of the Eastern school, which continued to influence the Italian illuminators up to the middle of the fifteenth century. But the *ornament* is, as I have just stated, perfectly original in general treatment, even if some of its features may be said to be derived from traditions of Greek art, which from Constantinople continued to influence that of Italy throughout the greater portion of the middle ages. Several MSS. of this singular and distinct style bear evidence of having been executed in Sicily. It is, therefore, possible that it may have originated there. The Normans found the Byzantine emperors still in possession of that island; and the union of Norman art with that of Byzantium, as practised in Sicily, may have produced this peculiar style—an hypothesis borne out to some extent by the singular effect wrought in the architecture of the country by the same combination. The description of the specimen, from the Bible of Pope Clement VII., will furnish farther details of this remarkably beautiful and distinct style of illumination.

Another style, also, was developed in Italy in the thirteenth and fourteenth centuries, during which some very fine MSS. were executed with large and striking miniatures, but of which the other ornaments were of a very subordinate character; in fact, merely decorative writing, consisting simply of initial letters, apparently executed entirely with the pen—the letters themselves being generally solid blue, surrounded and filled up with very delicate small open patterns in red, and terminating in the margin in long tails, like those in English

MSS. of the thirteenth century; only, instead of being solid, they are formed of light lines slightly enriched with simple and delicate penwork. A MS. in the British Museum (Royal, 6 E. ix.), executed about 1320, is a good example; and the Lansdowne MS. 463, also in the national collection, exhibits an English version of the style of somewhat later date.

For references to MSS. of the fourteenth century, see the appended list.

THE EARLY PART OF THE FIFTEENTH CENTURY.

Examples.—A PAGE FROM THE POEMS OF LYDGATE, B. M., HARL. 2278; A PAGE FROM QUEEN MARY'S BREVIARY, B. M. BIB. REG., 2 B. 15; AND A PAGE FROM ANOTHER MS. OF THE PERIOD, ALSO IN THE BRITISH MUSEUM; A PAGE FROM A FINE PSALTER IN THE POSSESSION OF MR. OWEN JONES; A PAGE FROM A MS. OF THE COMEDIES OF TERENCE, IN THE LIBRARY OF THE ARSENAL, PARIS; AND A PAGE FROM THE GREAT HOURS OF THE DUKE OF BERRI, IN THE BIBLIOTHEQUE NATIONALE, PARIS.

The style exhibited in the specimen from the poems of Lydgate may be said to be founded (like that of the Salisbury Lectionarium of the preceding century) on the rich style of the tenth century, which I have supposed to be the style of work known as the "Opus Anglicum." But in this specimen the foliage is not allowed to extend beyond the confining gold bars, that on the outside being unconnected with it. At the extremities, or corners, the design strongly resembles in principle that of the tenth century, on which it is founded; but it is more flowing, and branches off into exquisitely slight and graceful convolutions of quite a distinct character, forming in the whole design a figure similar to the ivy-leaf bracket of the fourteenth century, as will be observed on reference to the one we have given from "Les Merveilles du Monde." There are many connecting links of style between the ivy-leaf bracket and the present one; foliage somewhat similar to that of the last-mentioned style having been gradually introduced, increasing in richness towards the end of the fourteenth century; beautiful examples of which exist, executed during the reign of Edward III.

Another phase of the style represented by our specimen from the poems of Lydgate is exhibited in the magnificent page from the Psalter in the possession of Mr. Owen Jones. In my *description* of these two MSS. I have considered Mr. Jones' MS. to be a later amplification of the style of the Lydgate; but on mature consideration I think it possible that it may be the earlier style, as having greater analogy with that of the tenth century; for it will be found, on comparing it with the page from a Psalter of the tenth century which accompanies the page from the Devonshire Benedictional, that the proportions and principles of ornament of the general framework correspond very closely with that style, of which it is a magnificently modified reminiscence. These styles may be considered peculiar to English illumination, as well as that of the two following plates, which represent its next advance; in which the lighter extraneous portions are bounded by a ruled line, thus forming a regular and continuous border. This is the last period of the art of illumination of which English examples exist in any number. For after the temporary conquest of France by Henry V., the communication with the Continent became more intimate, and foreign artists practising more advanced styles were introduced in such numbers,

that native illuminators fell into disrepute, and from this period the finest illuminated MSS. may be said to have been exclusively executed on the Continent. Certainly after the reign of Henry VII. no important English examples occur, while it was after that date that the art attained (in finish and richness) its highest development on the Continent.

The last English style, just described, which had its closely allied styles on the Continent, appears to have been the immediate precursor, and in fact origin, of the well-known common border-patterns of the middle and latter portion of the fifteenth century, in which style great numbers of MSS. must have been executed; for the great bulk of the MS. missals and chronicles now existing exhibit that feeling; but this is not the place to treat of it in detail. An example will be found farther on, in a page from the Chronicles of England, and in its later phase, in two pages from a fragment of a missal in the possession of Mr. Owen Jones.

On the Continent, the ivy-leaf style, first exhibited in a very simple bracket, and then carried out into a complete border, as in the example from the "Hours of the Duke of Anjou," previously described, assumed towards the beginning of the fifteenth century a much more florid character; losing much of its original angularity. In fact, a distinct style was created in which the ivy-leaf feature (always gold) performs only a subordinate part, merely acting as a playful and glittering background to the more prominent parts of the composition, which is frequently full of design of the highest and richest character; as will be fully admitted on reference to our splendid example from the "Comedies of Terence." The style was partially foreshadowed in that of the principal pages of "Les Merveilles du Monde."

A specimen of a more regular and symmetrical variety of the style is our page from the truly magnificent "Great Hours of the Duke of Berri." From its more regular and *symmetrical* treatment, I infer that it is of somewhat earlier date,[*] though evidently of the same school as the Terence; for the tendency in art, both on the Continent and in England at this period, was to quit the symmetrical for the picturesque, evolving in architecture the style which has been termed "*flamboyant*," a term which might with equal propriety be applied to illuminations of the first period of transition towards the *picturesque* arrangement. For farther observations on the symmetrical variety of this period, see the description of the "Great Hours of the Duke of Berri."

From the ivy-leaf style was also developed another beautiful description of border, in which an inner and narrow strip of rich Gothic pattern branches out at the centre and corners into minute ramifications of the ivy branch, sometimes mixed with other features, partly in gold and partly in colours, which form themselves into a rich, deep, lace-like border of great regularity and beauty. Space does not permit my giving a specimen of this style, but a fine example may be seen in the exquisitely illuminated Prayer-book of Henry VI. in the British Museum, executed for him when a child, most likely in France, during the regency of the Duke of Bedford.[†] The miniatures of this little volume are probably the finest monuments of that branch of the art that the age produced. These last-mentioned styles are only found in

---

[*] A MS. evidently illuminated by the same hand is preserved in the public library of Brussels; it is known as the Prayer-book of the Duke Winceslaus of Luxemburgh, who died in 1383; so that this style may be perhaps more properly classed as one belonging to the end of the fourteenth century; though the illuminator probably lived and executed works for the Duke of Berri until his death in 1416.

[†] A specimen is given in Westwood's Palæogr. Sacr. Pict., pl. 32.

works executed on the Continent. The style of border, in which an inner border branches out at the extremities into the features that form the broad or exterior border, is well represented by our outline, No. 6½, from a MS. in the British Museum, Harl. No. 2900.

For references to MSS. of the fifteenth century, see the appended list.

THE MIDDLE OF THE FIFTEENTH CENTURY.

Examples.—A PAGE FROM "THE CHRONICLES OF ENGLAND," EXECUTED FOR EDWARD IV., AND TWO PAGES FROM A MISSAL IN THE POSSESSION OF MR. OWEN JONES.

The ivy-leaf style, and those founded upon flowing foliage, were combined about the middle of the fifteenth century to form a style in which an immense number of illuminated MSS. were produced, as stated at page 8. In this combination, the *symmetrical* arrangement was abandoned for one that may be termed *picturesque*, irregular portions of the border being alternately occupied by the ivy pattern, and purple or variously-coloured scroll-work, formed of the flowing foliage above alluded to. This arrangement necessitated the occasional restoration of the frequently lost balance of strength; for which purpose, the profuse employment of gold spots surrounded by a circular black line with radiating lines of black was resorted to, producing a quaint, sparkling, and pleasing effect. This device had been made use of before, in the pure ivy-leaf bracket period, but very sparingly; it was now so profusely employed in filling up the spaces between the ramifications of the pattern, that it positively became a sort of background of spangles, and produced a peculiarly glittering effect. Figures were also arbitrarily introduced in the midst of the arabesque patterns, standing on little islands of green turf, or fanciful rock-work, and their place was sometimes occupied by quaintly-designed monsters and nondescript insects or reptiles. The ivy-leaf portion was farther varied by the introduction of branches of different plants, among which those of most frequent occurrence are the daisy, the columbine, the strawberry, the rose, and occasionally the vine and the mulberry. This was the period, too, when heraldic blazonry began to be introduced with effect as a leading feature in illuminated borders, almost every illuminated book exhibiting in the border of the first page the armorial bearings of the person for whom it was executed. Of the general characteristics of this period, the large page from the Chronicles of England, executed for Edward IV., is a good general example. It does not afford, however, an accurate idea of the minute and intricate work of the smaller missals executed at that time. The inner lines of burnished gold of these little Prayer-books—their inner solid border, from which the principal initial of the page is sometimes made to issue in a very artistic manner, and their open fillagree border of intricate ramifications of various foliage, similar in style to our page from the Chronicles of England, but infinitely more minute and careful in treatment, combined with their numerous highly-wrought miniatures, give them a rich, quaint, and glittering air of artistic elaboration, that will cause them to be sought by the curious in matters of art, as long as the durable vellum on which they are written shall resist the slow but inevitable inroads of time. Missals of this style are so common, in consequence of the vast numbers which were executed in Flanders, especially at Bruges, where their production became in fact a branch of manufacture, that every person in the slightest degree inte-

rested in the art of illumination has seen many specimens; I have, therefore, in the limited space of this work, not thought it necessary to give one. But of the ultimate development of the style, when the larger foliated portions became more equally distributed, towards the end of the century, I have given a remarkably fine specimen from a fragment of a missal in the possession of Mr. Owen Jones, which is the latest form of *open* border previous to the general introduction of *back-grounds*, which will be the next step of the art to examine, after saying a few words upon the *open* borderings of the Italian illuminators of the middle of the fifteenth century.

For references to MSS. of the fifteenth century, see the appended list.

THE ITALIAN ILLUMINATIONS OF THE MIDDLE OF THE FIFTEENTH CENTURY.

Examples. — PAGE FROM THE ORATIONS OF DEMOSTHENES, A MS. IN THE BRITISH MUSEUM, A PAGE FROM A MS. JUVENAL, IN THE BRITISH MUSEUM, HARL. 2730, AND A PAGE FROM A MS. AULUS GELLIUS, ALSO IN THE BRITISH MUSEUM, BURNEY MSS. NO. 175.

The Italian illuminations of this period, like those of the North, are frequently composed of alternating portions of light, and more massive ornament. But a great line of distinction is to be drawn between them in one particular, namely, that of symmetry; for while the more Northern illuminators abandoned the symmetrical arrangement for one of a picturesque character, the Italians continued to preserve the symmetry of their compositions, introducing medallions, and other extraneous features of enrichment, with great artistic skill, and without disturbing the symmetrical feeling, and making them appear, as it were, a part of the general ornament; so well is their introduction made to *dovetail* and harmonize with the lighter features of the open bordering. Of this style, the specimen page from the MS. Orations of Demosthenes is a very pleasing example, and the tablet for the title is a very interesting Italianised version of the Byzantine capping, or heading, which, as already stated in page 1, is the only striking feature in Greek illumination.

But another remarkably distinct style was developed and perfected at this period in Italy. I allude to the style formed of white interlacing branches, the interstices of which are filled with various colours, generally blue, red, green, and violet, symmetrically balanced, and generally powdered with white dots arranged in triangles. This style is beautifully exhibited in our specimen from the MS. Juvenal, which is a somewhat late example of the style; the interlacings being interrupted by the introduction of compartments containing miniatures, &c., and armorial bearings, beautifully executed, of the Roman Cardinal for whom the book was executed; while in earlier specimens, the interlacing is generally uninterrupted throughout the border, and of a somewhat simpler, or rather, more monotonous character; the extremely quaint and unexpected turnings and curves being confined to later works. Some books in this style have only large initial letters, which are frequently extremely beautiful; and sometimes only a simple gold ground. Other MSS. have a marginal bar only, of ornament of this style, from which in some instances the principal initial letter is made, as it were, to grow, in a very ingenious and beautiful manner. Some artists treating this style have endeavoured to overcome the objection that might be offered to a continued series of curves, by the introduction of straight

D

17

branches, occurring at regular distances, and alternately leaning to the right and then to the left—an innovation that has a peculiarly crisp and decisive effect.

The highest degree of enrichment to which this style was carried, is finely exhibited in our magnificent specimen from a MS. of Aulus Gellius in the British Museum. These ultimate enrichments consist in colouring the interlacing branches themselves in alternate masses of blue, green, red, or violet, heightened with gold. In these cases it became necessary to change the character of the background, which instead of being varied in colour, as when the interlacing branches were white, now became either black, or gold; in some cases producing the most gorgeous possible effect; of which our specimen is an example, though some imperfections in the printing prevent it from completely conveying all the exquisite beauty of the original.

I have not space for a coloured specimen of a remarkable and ingenious variation of the two last-mentioned styles which arose in Italy about the same time, and was formed by using, instead of branches, interweaving *cables*, which admitted of still greater symmetry and regularity of arrangement, and was consequently highly acceptable to the Italian illuminators, by whom these features were always carefully cultivated. This cable-work, like the branch-work, was first white, but afterwards richly coloured. Of the white period, a MS. Petrarch in the British Museum, Harl. 3517, is a good specimen; and of the coloured period, the celebrated Pliny of the Bodleian Library is a most resplendent example. The two outlines, Nos. 7 and 8, are examples. There are one or two examples of this style in the British Museum, Additional MSS. 1479 and 14,815.

For references to other MSS. in these styles see the appended list.

Another peculiar Italian style of the fifteenth century was one in which the ornament consisted merely of a marginal bar, somewhat less than an inch in breadth, formed of an exterior broad gold edging, and filled up with richly-coloured foliage of great variety of design. In Flemish and French illumination, when the ornament was confined to a broad band of ornament in the exterior margins only—like our pages from the Prayer-book of Henry VII.—they were left square at top and bottom; but the more fastidious Italians shaded off, as it were, the abrupt finish of this solid bar, by making it terminate in a medallion containing a portrait or circular ornament, which medallion was blended into the margin of plain vellum by means of slight and delicate ornaments which were made to radiate from it, terminating in a light tuft of open arabesque foliage. In other instances an exterior marginal ornament was formed of a central slender gold bar, from which light and feathering foliage was made to issue at intervals from a sort of husk or cup, the intervals between the bolder leafage being filled with delicately-pencilled single black lines, occasionally terminating in a gold spot surrounded with a black line. Of the former of these two styles, the outline, No. 9, is a good example, from the fine copy of Pliny's Natural History, *printed* at Venice in 1476, the ornaments of which are illuminated by hand. It is now in the Bodleian Library, Oxford.

For references to other Italian MSS., see the appended list.

THE ITALIAN CHORAL BOOKS.

The gigantic initials to the enormous choral books of some of the churches of Italy, must not here be passed over without remark; though, as they seldom extend into decorative borders, they hardly come within the plan of my work. Some of them are of truly enormous dimensions, being above a foot in height. Those of the fifteenth century are generally composed of blue and green foliage formed of acanthus leaves, with portions of a scale-like pattern, generally of deep carmine, the whole relieved with gold. These letters, when of earlier periods, those of the thirteenth and fourteenth centuries, for instance, are generally composed of ornaments of similar character to those exhibited in our specimen from the Bible of Pope Clement. But those of both early and late periods almost invariably enclose a large miniature picture, sometimes executed by the first masters of the age. The large C appended to our description of the MS. Roman History of the Library of the Arsenal, Paris, will give some idea of the common style of these letters in the fifteenth century; especially if the broad plain portion of pinkish red, only ornamented with small white rings and lines, be supposed to be composed of a rich scaly pattern of carmine, shaded with a still deeper tone of the same colour. The two outline specimens are farther examples—the former (No. 9) of the fourteenth century, from a manuscript mentioned in Dibdin's Decameron, the latter (No. 10) of the fifteenth century, from a MS. in the British Museum.

THE BYZANTINE STYLE IN THE FIFTEENTH CENTURY.

Example.—TWO PAGES FROM A GREEK MS. OF THE GOSPELS OF THE FIFTEENTH CENTURY IN THE BRITISH MUSEUM, HARLEIAN COLLECTION.

I have introduced one specimen of Greek art of this period, to show how little the disposition of ornament and general arrangement of design had varied in that channel of the art of illumination. The specimen, though executed in Italy, is the work of a Greek artist, probably an emigrant from the fast-falling Byzantine capital. Constantinople afforded no longer the advantages which a great and luxurious city generally offers to artists of all descriptions, and it was now principally in the Greek Islands, and in Italy, that her illuminators continued to practise their art. There is, in the Bibliothèque Nationale of Paris, a MS. executed in the Island of Rhodes as late as the middle of the sixteenth century, which bears all the usual characteristics of the Byzantine manner. This style of art appears to have followed the track of its parent, the Greek Church, being still practised in parts of Russia with all the old conventional forms of ornament. These appear to be followed with a sort of veneration and accuracy truly extraordinary—the very forms and combinations of the tenth, twelfth, and thirteenth centuries being reproduced in the present day with all the correctness and care that marked the works of those early periods. M. Papeti, in 1846,* found the monks of Mount Athos still practising the art from ancient models, and from an ancient book of rules, in which the most minute directions were given for every detail of costume of every saint in the Greek calendar.†

For list of Greek MSS. of the seventh and subsequent century, see the appended list.

* " Salon de 1846, par Theophile Gaultier."
† This work has been translated and published by M. Didron.

ILLUMINATIONS OF THE END OF THE FIF-TEENTH CENTURY, AND THE BEGINNING OF THE SIXTEENTH.

Examples. — TWO PAGES FROM THE PRAYER-BOOK OF HENRY VII., B. M., BIBL. REG. 2, D. XL, THREE PAGES FROM THE "HOURS OF ANNE OF BRITTANY" IN THE BIBL. NAT., PARIS, AND TWO PAGES FROM THE CALENDAR OF A RICH MISSAL IN THE LIBRARY OF THE ARSENAL, PARIS.

In the middle of the fifteenth century, the leading characteristic of illuminated borders, as distinguished from those of the latter portion of the century, was, that they were in almost all cases formed of *open* work, that is, having no background; which last-named feature, a background, became general towards the end of the century. The first step towards a general solid background, was its partial adoption. A line was drawn, generally a diagonal one, separating the light ivy-leaf portion of the pattern from that formed of more massive foliage, and the ground beneath the latter was filled by gold, blue, or some positive colour; while the ground of the lighter portion of the ornament remained white. These alternations of rich masses of colour, and delicate open fillagree have sometimes a very striking effect, though not founded on sound artistic principles, and would be very dangerous to imitate in modern works without very skilful modification. Sometimes the respective spaces of solid and open work were of pleasing forms, such as the quarterfoil, &c., &c.; sometimes a serpentine line, touching each side of the border, separated the compartments, which was perhaps the most pleasing form under which these patchwork borders appeared. As this is not to be considered a perfect style, but merely a transition, I have not given a specimen; and proceed to describe the adoption of complete backgrounds.

The first style with a solid background that I shall describe, is one in which the conventional foliage, originally founded upon the acanthus-leaf, is so artistically blended with the forms of common and well-known plants, that they appear to belong naturally to each other. In the earliest of these compositions the conventional foliage predominates, and natural flowers issue from it with the graceful ease of nature, producing a very charming effect; of which the outline specimen (No. 12) from a missal in the Soane Museum, illuminated by Lucas von Leyden, is a fine example. In some examples of works of the class, the natural flower predominates, and forms the basis of the composition, from which conventional foliage of a florid heraldic character is made to issue with beautiful effect. Of this latter style, our specimen pages from the Prayer-book of Henry VII. form exquisite examples. Part of the advantage of this introduction of highly-coloured extraneous foliage grafted on that of a natural plant, is, that the lower portions, where green would have unpleasantly predominated, are thus rendered equally attractive in colour with the upper or flower-bearing portions of the plant.

This direction of the art towards the adoption of purely natural forms was soon carried to its highest pitch, and illuminations were shortly produced in which all conventional ornament whatever was abandoned, and natural flowers and fruits ornamentally and yet architectonically treated, formed the only features of decoration. In the "Hours of Anne of Brittany" this feeling was carried out in the most beautiful manner. I have stated in reference to the borders of the Prayer-book of Henry VII., that in the lower portion of the plants, where *green* would have predominated too strongly for the decorative purposes of the illuminator, that imaginary foliage of arbitrary design, both as to form and colour, was introduced, with a view to restoring the balance of colour disturbed by the richer tones of the flowering portion of the plant. In the "Hours of Anne of Brittany," the artist has struck out a much more exquisite device for the same purpose. The lower portions of the plants being studded with richly-coloured insects, in natural positions: a fluttering butterfly of dazzling tints, here enriching a too soberly-toned portion of the design; and there, a gorgeous beetle, like a creeping jewel, giving more than the effect of a flower to some other part where the predominance of the green would have been monotonous. Our examples from this beautiful book are insufficient to convey an idea of the variety and splendour of its three or four hundred illuminated pages; but they will serve to illustrate sufficiently the principles of the style here alluded to. One of which, especially distinctive of the works of the end of the fifteenth and beginning of the sixteenth centuries, is the elaborately wrought and richly toned *shadows* by which the objects, whether on a gold or a richly-coloured ground, are made to stand out from it with an effect sometimes almost deceptive. The high finish and intensity of the rich brown shadows to the plants in the "Hours of Anne of Brittany," are quite remarkable features of that exquisite work.

Sometimes, in seeking after novelty, the artists of the beginning of the sixteenth century made the main branchwork of their foliage form separate and symmetrical compartments, which were respectively filled with different colours. The famous Missal, by Hemling, now in the British Museum (No. 17,280), contains one or two rich examples of this style. Such were the leading styles that distinguished the end of the fifteenth, and first half of the sixteenth century, and many modifications, and some distinct though inferior styles, existed, of which I have not taken note, and in fact which the extent and plan of the present work would not admit of; but I may here mention that this period, especially from 1480 to 1530, was the great period of heraldic embellishments in illumination; these features being treated, especially in the German schools, with the most elaborate design, and sometimes most splendid effect. Neither must I omit to mention a style which originated in the beginning of the sixteenth century, which consisted of separate flowers strewed carelessly, but with some attention to balance of effect, over a richly-coloured ground. Of this style our specimens from the calendar of the rich Missal, in the Library of the Arsenal, are good examples. Other objects than flowers were soon introduced in borders of this feeling, which became great favourites with the amateurs of the day. The first features thus mingled with the flowers were single feathers, of rich colouring; then birds' nests, birds, animals, and eventually, as the art declined, jewels, and other objects of trivial and unartistic character.

For references to MSS. of the end of fifteenth and beginning of sixteenth century, see the appended list.

PICTURE BORDERS.—BEGINNING OF THE SIXTEENTH CENTURY.

Example.—A PAGE FROM THE "HOURS OF ANNE OF FRANCE," IN THE BIBLIOTHEQUE NATIONALE, PARIS.

Towards the beginning of the sixteenth century, amongst other strainings after novelty indicative of the period, that of compressing pictures into thin slips to form borders, was perhaps one of the most remarkable. Our specimen page, from the (so-called) "Hours of Anne of France," exhibits this arrangement in a favourable manner; part of the lateral border being filled by ornament, and so giving the picture a better proportion, while the space allotted to the lower picture is sufficiently deep to make the proportion agreeable. In some instances, the picture at the side reaches to the top, whilst very large figures are forced into it, producing an unpleasant and crushed effect; of this class is an otherwise fine MS. lately in the possession of Mr. H. Bohn, but now in the library of Lord Ashburton. The calendar of the "Hours of Anne of Brittany" is one of the earliest examples of this feeling of converting a picture into a border; but it is, perhaps, one of the most successful ones; for the picture (enclosed in a simple gold band) is supposed to occupy the whole page, leaving of course a proper margin, whilst a tablet is placed in the centre of the picture, also bordered with gold, and this tablet receives the text; care being taken in designing the picture to keep all the essential features of the composition *outside* of the space occupied by the tablet, thus producing at once a complete picture, and yet the effect of a border. As, for instance, in a picture representing a landscape with figures, the figures occupy the bottom and part of the sides of the border, whilst the upper part of the sides, and top, are filled in with trees, mountains, and sky; the middle distance of the picture being, as it were, hidden by the centre tablet.

ILLUMINATIONS IN CAMÉE-GRIS, OF THE FIFTEENTH AND BEGINNING OF THE SIXTEENTH CENTURY.

Example.—TWO PAGES FROM THE DIALOGUES OF FRANCIS I. AND JULIUS CÆSAR, B. M., HARL., 6205.

In my description of the two pages from the Dialogues of Francis I. and Cæsar, I have said all that appears necessary (in this brief treatment of the subject) on the origin and practice of executing illuminations in camaïeu or camée-gris, and grisaille, as the two varieties are sometimes termed. It arose, no doubt, from a feeling that all the effects that could be obtained by the arrangement of rich colours had been worked out, or abused; and novelty and repose was consequently sought in a delicate monochrome treatment. There are many examples of florid borderings treated in this manner; and also very large miniatures, in which the heightening of the general effect, by means of a few objects richly coloured, has not, as in our example, been resorted to.

For references to examples of this style, see the appended list.

ITALIAN ILLUMINATIONS OF THE END OF THE FIFTEENTH AND BEGINNING OF THE SIXTEENTH CENTURIES.

Examples.—A PAGE FROM THE MS. ROMAN HISTORY IN THE LIBRARY OF THE ARSENAL, PARIS, AND TWO PAGES AND A BORDER FROM THE MS. ILLUMINATED BY GUILIO CLOVIO, IN THE SOANE MUSEUM.

In Italy, as in the North, *backgrounds* to the borders were gradually adopted towards the end of the fifteenth

century, generally of gold, but sometimes, as in the Flemish and German examples, of rich colours. But still the *picturesque* arrangement of the Flemish and German artists was rarely resorted to, the *symmetry* of the previous Italian styles being firmly adhered to as a general principle. The Arabesque style, founded by Raphael upon the remains of Roman frescoes, was that principally followed, in various forms; in some cases delicately slender in general treatment, in others, almost overcharged with richness. A magnificent specimen of a medium feeling is our example from the MS. Roman history of the Library of the Arsenal. But a distinct school was eventually founded by Girolamo and Francesco dai Libri, and carried to its utmost perfection by Giulio Clovio, in which the pure Arabesque was nearly abandoned, and the borders were formed by elaborate compositions of large allegorical figures, groups of armour and other trophies, imitations of engraved cameos, highly-wrought imitations of strings of pearls, detached gems of rich colour, and other similar objects. These features were interspersed with medallion miniatures, armorial bearings, and other extraneous materials; all, however, generally blended into a very harmonious and rich general composition. Our magnificent specimens of two pages from the MS. illuminated by Giulio Clovio, in the Soane Museum, form fine examples of the style, though some of the smaller missals of the period exceed it in minute beauty of detail and richness of effect—that by Girolamo dai Libri, in the Bodleian Library, being perhaps the finest in existence, though the Clovio MS. in the private Royal Library of the King of Naples has the reputation of surpassing every other production of the art of illumination, but the jealous care with which it is preserved prevents the opportunity of even examining it at leisure, much more of making a copy of any of its reputed marvellous pages.

ILLUMINATED DIPLOMAS.

Example.—THE FRONTISPIECE OF AN ILLUMINATED DIPLOMA IN THE BRITISH MUSEUM.

In Venice it was the practice to illuminate in a very rich manner the first page of the diplomas granted to every governor of a Venetian dependency, on his appointment. In the fifteenth and sixteenth centuries, some of these illuminations were of a very high character of art; it being part of the duties of the painter of the Republic for the time being, to paint the principal portion. The one I have given as an example is a work of the sixteenth century, and the miniature was formerly supposed to be a late production of the hand of Titian, who was painter to the Republic at or near that period. The excellency of the work affords some support to the hypothesis. The border, or rather frame, is in a very grand style of ornament, in the same feeling as some of the magnificent ceilings of the ducal palace, executed about that time.

THE SPANISH SCHOOL OF ILLUMINATION.

The Spanish style of illumination ought, perhaps, to have found a place here, had space permitted, but I have not attempted to separate the French, Flemish, and German schools, as they all followed pretty nearly the same course; and the Spanish (with the exception of a Moresque character, produced by the horse-shoe arch in the architectural features of early illuminations) followed a very similar routine of

development to that of the other countries of Western Europe. The last specimens being illuminations of printed books as late as the middle of the seventeenth century, in a debased but brilliant style, one example of which, a most superb specimen, was destroyed by the unfortunate fire which consumed the fine library at Hafod.

THE CHARACTER OF ILLUMINATIONS AT THE END OF THE SIXTEENTH, AND DURING THE SEVENTEENTH CENTURY.

Example.—A PAGE FROM THE PRAYER-BOOK OF LOUIS XIV.

It may be conceived that the wide extension of the perfected art of printing, which, even in the beginning of the sixteenth century, had become very general, would have entirely stopped the development of those of the scribe and illuminator; but this was far from being the case. The first quarter of the sixteenth century was the most prolific in examples of illuminations of the richest class; and even until the commencement of the seventeenth, the art continued to be practised with success. A style derived from that of Lucas von Leyden and his followers, much overloaded with ornament, was practised as late as 1601, of which the celebrated St. Croix Missal, in the British Museum, is an elaborate example.

A more chaste style, however, grew up among the higher class of illuminators, and books executed for Francis I. of France, and his immediate successors, generally exhibit a subdued tone of colouring and design, which was probably very attractive after the almost over-wrought richness of the styles that had preceded it. Some of the borders of this period have a gold ground, subdued in its brightness by a wash of light brown, on which chaste decorations are sparingly introduced in bright gold, relieved with a deep brown, such as interlacing initials in a style approaching the modern cursive manner; scrolls for mottoes, occasionally surmounted by the coronet, crown, or arms of the person for whom the book was illuminated, the whole executed in different tones of gold and brown; sometimes relieved under the outside of the gold border by a delicately-executed shadow of ultramarine on the plain vellum. In Italy, a simpler style was also gradually adopted among the superior illuminators, of which a fine example may be seen in the well-known Missal of the King Sigismund of Poland, now in the British Museum.*

Illuminations were also executed in printed books from the very commencement of the art of printing, so that the finest examples of the art of illumination, after the middle of the fifteenth century, are not always confined to MSS., but are frequently to be found in printed books — the noble Bible of Fust and Scheffer, being one of the earliest and finest examples, of which a beautiful copy is preserved in the British Museum; the capital letters of this book exhibit some of the finest examples of German illumination of the period. Another (imperfect), carried to Venice for the purpose, has the illuminated letters in the Italian manner. The life of Francesco Sforza, *printed* on vellum, and exquisitely illuminated by Girolamo dai Libri, is another Italian example of the alliance of the arts of printing and illumination. It was the presentation copy of the work to Cardinal Sforza,

* Formerly in the Collection of the late Duke of Sussex. Westwood, Pal. Sacr. Pict., pl. 36.

and the original gorgeous binding is still perfect. It was bequeathed to the British Museum, with the most valuable portion of his splendid library, by the late Mr. Grenville. A splendid volume, printed on vellum, and illuminated by Herrera, for Philip IV. of Spain, as late as 1637, was one of the most elaborate and beautiful specimens of the art. It formed part of Mr. Johnes' celebrated library at Hafod, and was unfortunately destroyed by fire, with nearly the whole of the other literary treasures there collected. But examples of illumination in printed books do not come within the scope of the plan of this work, and some of the rich styles which mark the decadence of the art, are not sufficiently distinct to demand a specimen in illustration. The last style of all, however, that which originated in France in the reign of Louis XIV., though far from being a good or pure style, is yet so distinct as to require an illustrative example in this work.

It is founded on the style of art generally known in France as the "Genre Versaille," and originated in the florid pencils, and still more exuberant fancies, of Le Brun and Le Pautre. Its minute peculiarities will be found detailed in the description of our specimen-page from the Prayer-book of Louis XIV. A specimen of the style, truly magnificent from its dimensions, being nearly three feet in height, is the famous Rouen Missal, completed as late as 1682, after having occupied its illuminator thirty years in its execution. It is shown in the public library of that city.

But it may be taken as a general rule that no illuminations of any consequence were executed after about 1650. French books were, however, still occasionally illuminated, though in a weaker and weaker style of gradually sinking art, till the middle of the eighteenth century; but after 1780, the revolutionary politics of France, seeking the ancient Republics of Greece and Rome as their standard of excellence, were followed by the fine arts; and as the remains of classical art offered no examples of the art of illumination, that beautiful branch of design became extinct. Thus, the intricate and beautiful school of art which had been developed with wonderful originality and variety throughout the whole of the middle ages now died away, and was, except by a few enthusiastic antiquaries, forgotten. The only style of general art in vogue was that founded on crude and meagre imitations of the worst classical models, producing, as practised, the most wretched effect on the art of other schools: for a French supremacy in art seems to have been acknowledged without dispute throughout Europe. This feeling of crudely copying antique art existed with more or less intensity till about 1820, when a reaction as extraordinary again took place; the works of the middle ages, and even the worst specimens of the worst periods, being sought with great avidity. This taste continued to extend, and within the last few years became a lamentable mania; the most servile imitations of the bad drawing, the crude combinations, and even the rude finishing, being considered evident marks of the most accomplished taste. A better feeling is now rising; the finest features of the art of any age are alone considered worthy of study or reproduction; and beautiful works of the middle ages are sought, not for the purpose of making close and servile copies of them with all their defects, but of studying the *principles* upon which they were composed, and with those principles producing works more in accordance with the spirit and sympathies of the present age, than the works of any former era can possibly afford.

Such a series as the present will therefore not only afford gratification to the general amateur, from the beauty, intricacy,

E

and variety of its successive examples, beautifully exhibiting the course and progress of an exquisite branch of decorative art for above a thousand years, but will afford to artists in that department a body of original and ingenius combinations of form, colour, and general effect, such as no single imagination could ever realise, and upon which—by carefully studying the principles of composition rather than their superficial effect—they may found new designs in accordance with the great advance of other branches of modern civilization, and which will, thus treated, have the advantage of being as original as the beautiful but quaint compositions on which they are founded.

For references to MSS. of the sixteenth and seventeenth centuries, see the following list.

H. N. H.

LIST OF SOME OF THE

MOST REMARKABLE ILLUMINATED BOOKS OF THE MIDDLE AGES.

Greek and Latin MSS. of the Fourth, Fifth, and Sixth Centuries.

Pages from all the MSS. marked * are figured in this work, and the Manuscripts marked B.M., are in the British Museum.

The Codex purpureo-argenteus of Ulphilas, written in the year 360, preserved at Upsal, in Sweden.

The Codex argenteo-purpureus Cæsareo Vindobonensis, or purple and gold Book of Genesis at Vienna (Greek). This remarkable MS. has been described by Lambecius, Nesselius, Hollarius, Montfaucon, Holmes, Adle, Horne, Dibdin, and Agincourt.

The Golden Greek Canons of Eusebius, B.M., MSS. Add. 5111.

The Iliad of St. Mark's, Venice, published in fac-simile by Villoisin (Greek).

The Iliad of the Ambrosian Library at Milan, published by Card. Mai (Greek).

The two MSS. of Dioscorides at Vienna (Greek).

The Roman Calendar at Vienna (Latin).

The Vatican Virgil, No. 3225 (Latin). The British Museum possesses a volume of fac-similes copied by Bartoli from this MS. MS. Lansd., 834.

The Great Virgil of St. Denis, formerly in the Vatican, No. 3867 (Latin).

The Gospels of St. Augustine (Latin), Corpus Christi College, Cambridge, No. 286.

The Psalter in the Vatican, fifth or sixth century, No. 1209 (Greek).

Fragments of St. Matthew's and St. John's Gospel, in silver on purple vellum. B.M., Cot., Titus C. xv. (Greek).

A Greek Bible (known as the Alexandrian MS.), supposed to be of the fourth century.

The Book of Genesis, nearly destroyed by fire, but finely restored by Mr. Gough, highly illuminated, and supposed to be earlier than the Alexandrian MS., B. M., Cot. Otho B. vi. (Greek).

The purple Gospels, in letters of silver, of the church of Perugia, sixth century (Latin).*

Fragment of the Book of Kings, at Vienna, sixth century (Latin).

The Gospels of St. Germain, Bib. Nat. 663, entirely in golden letters, sixth century (Latin).

The Codex Turinensis, portion of Psalms, Royal Library, Turin, on extremely thin purple vellum, in silver letters.

Palimpsest MS., in Trinity College, Dublin, Book of Isaiah, &c., &c., on purple vellum, sixth century.

* Only about six fine Greek MSS. on purple vellum are known.

The Gallican latin Psalter, date, A.D. 576, now in Bib. Nat., Paris.

Greek MSS. of Seventh and subsequent Centuries.

Although I have not treated of the Byzantine school of illumination in this work, the following list of richly illuminated MSS. in that style of art may be acceptable.

Commentaries of Gregory Nazianzen, ninth century, Bib. Nat. de Paris, Gr. 510.

Greek Psalter, with commentary, tenth century, Bib. Nat. de Paris, Gr. 139.

The Ebnerian Codex, twelfth century, in Mr. Douce's Coll., Bodleian Library, Oxford (Greek).

The Canonici MSS., Nos. 92, 103, and 110 in the Bodleian Library (Greek).

Poems of Anacreon, tenth century, published in fac-simile by Spaletti, mentioned in Dibdin's Decameron. A series of fac-similes is in the library of the Royal Institution. (Greek).

The Greek Gospels, eleventh century, B. M., Harleian Lib., No. 1810.

Greek Gospels, eleventh century, B. M., additional 5107.

History of Joshua, with drawings, in the Vatican Library, No. 405 (Greek). Agincourt.

The Menologium or Martyrology, with 430 drawings, in the Vatican Library, No. 1613 (Greek). Agincourt.

Christian Topography of Cosmus, in the Vatican Library, No. 699 (Greek). Agincourt.

Commentary on Isaiah, in the Vatican Library, No. 775 (Greek). Agincourt.

Hippocrates, in the library of S. Lorenzo, Florence, eleventh century (Greek). Agincourt.

Greek MS., twelfth century, Bibl. Nat., Paris, No. 543.

Greek Homilies, twelfth century, in the Vatican Library, No. 1162.

Gospels of the Emperor John Comnenus II., in the Vatican Library, No. 2 (Greek).

Greek Bible, fourteenth century, in the library of the Vatican, No. 746.

The Gospels of St. Luke and St. John, in golden letters, in the Vatican, No. 50, eighth century.

Greek MS., B. M., Arundel 27, an Evangelistiarium, a fine specimen of Greek caligraphy of the ninth or tenth century.

Greek MS., B. M., Harl. 2908.

B. M., Burney MSS., 19 and 20, of twelfth and thirteenth centuries. The additional MSS. in the same library, 11836, 1130, and 4950-51, are also specimens of Byzantine art of the eleventh and twelfth centuries.

A list of some of the more remarkable MSS. of the Irish, and Anglo-Saxon schools resembling the Irish, of the Sixth or Seventh, to the Tenth Century.

The Book of Kells, in the library of Trinity College, Dublin.

The Gospels of St. Columba, in the same library.

Archbishop Usher's Gospels, in the same library.

The Book of Armagh, now in the collection of the Royal Irish Academy.

The Gospels of Mac Durnan, in the library of the Archbishop of Canterbury.

The Gospels of Mac Regol, or the Rushworth Book, in the Bodleian Library, Oxford.

The Gospels of Lindisfarne, or Durham Book, seventh century, B. M., Cotton., Nero, D. 4.*

The Gospels of St. Chad, in the library of Litchfield Cathedral.

The Gospel of St. John, in Corp. Christi College, Cambridge.

The Gospels in the library of Durham Cathedral.

The purple Gospels, in the Royal Library, Stockholm.

The Gospels of St. John, late in the library at Stowe, seventh century.

Psalter said to have belonged to King Orwin, eleventh or twelfth century, B. M., Galba, A. v.

Gospels written by St. Mulling, Trinity College, Dublin.

MS. in B. M., Otho C. v. ; fragment of Gospels, seventh or eighth century.

The MSS. of the Gospels, in the library of St. Gall, in Switzerland.

The Gospels, No. 108, of the ancient library of St. Germain des Prés, supposed to be at St. Petersburgh.

The Latin Gospels, Bibl. Nat. de Paris, No. 693.

The Pontificale, Bibl. Nat. de Paris, No. 943.

The Psalter of St. Augustine, B. M. Cotton. Vesp. A. 1.

The Gospels (being portion of the Biblia Gregoriana), B. M. MS. Reg., 1 E. 6.

The Psalter in the library of St. John's College, Cambridge.

The Psalter of King Alfred [?], late in the Duke of Buckingham's library.

The Psalter of St. Ouen, in the Public Library, Rouen.

The Psalter of Ricemarchus, in the library of Trinity College, Dublin.

The small Gospels, Bibl. Harl. MSS., No. 1802 and 1023.

The Gospels of St. Kilien, discovered in his tomb, preserved at Wurtzburgh.

Missal of St. Columbanus, Ambrosian Library, Milan.

The Leabhor Dhimma, Trinity College, Dublin.

The Hymns of St. Patrick, in the same library.

Copy of Lactantius, Royal Library, Turin.

Most of these MSS. contain pure specimens of the Irish style ; a few, however, are of various and mixed styles—some slightly resembling the Gallican and Merovingian styles, of which specimens may be seen in the work of Count Bastard.

A list of Anglo-Saxon MSS., from the Eighth or Ninth to the Eleventh or Twelfth Century.

Cotton. MS.—Cleopatra, C. viii., Prudentius, with 83 illustrations, tenth or eleventh century.

,, Titus, C. xvi., another copy of Prudentius, 46 outline drawings, eleventh or twelfth century, Anglo-Saxon art.

,, Claudius, B. iv., Alfric's Anglo-Saxon Paraph. on the Pentateuch and Joshua, profusely illustrated, tenth or eleventh century.

,, Julius, A. vi., a fine Anglo-Saxon Calendar, entirely copied by Shaw, eleventh century.

,, Nero, C. iv., a Psalter of about twelfth century.

,, Tiberius, B. v. (Pt. I.), Varia Historica et Astronomica, upwards of 50 illustrations, Anglo-Saxon art.

,, Tiberius, C. vi., Latin and Anglo-Saxon Psalter, a fine MS., with paintings, tenth century.

Cotton. M.S.—Titus, D. xxvii., Tractatus varii plerumque Saxonici, exquisitely written, but few illustrations in outline. A curious volume, tenth or eleventh century.

,, Vespasian, A. viii., Book of Grants by King Edgar to the Abbey of Winchester, written in letters of gold, A.D. 966.

In the Public Library at Cambridge,, the Book of Genesis, in Anglo-Norman hand, in Corpus Christi College, Cambridge, S. 18, N. 78.

Extract from Alfric's Genesis, in Lincoln Library.

Fragments of Alfric's Heptateuch, in Corpus Christi College.

Psalter in the University Library of Cambridge, F. f. 1, 23, eleventh century.

In Bodl. Lib., Junius 27, a Psalter, tenth century.

In Brit. Mus. Bibl. Reg., 2 B., v., Psalter, tenth century.

Harl. M.S., 603, Latin Psalter, Anglo-Saxon illustrations, eleventh century.

Cotton MS., Otho, C. i.

Bibl. Reg. 1. A. xiv., eleventh century, in Norman-Saxon.

Precationes et Rationes, in linguâ Saxonicâ, a beautiful MS., Bibl. Reg. 2 B. V.

MS. in Bodl. Lib. (Bibl. Hatton, 56), " De Officio Missæ," written in Anglo-Saxon or Irish character, eighth century.

Charlemagne, or Caroline MSS. of the Eighth and Ninth Centuries.

The Evangelistarium of Charlemagne, upon purple vellum, in the library of the Louvre.

The Psalter given to Charlemagne by Pope Hadrian, at Vienna.

Gospels with Miniatures, eighth century, in the library of St. Genevieve, Paris (Waagen).

The MSS. in Bibl. Nat., Paris, numbered S. L. 626, A. F. 281, 2110, 2606, and 2769.

The Charlemagne Gospels of St. Riquier in the Public Library of Abbeville.

The Charlemagne Gospels in the Public Library of Treves.

The Codex Witikindi, in the Royal Library, Berlin.

The Purple Gospels, found on the knees of Charlemagne when his tomb was opened, supposed to be at Berlin or Vienna. (Casley's catalogue).

The Golden Gospels of Charles the Bald, in the Royal Library, Munich.

The Golden Gospels of the Harleian Library, No. 2788.*

The Golden Gospels of St. Medard, of Soissons, Bibl. Nat., Paris, S. L.686.

The Bible of St. Paul at Rome, now in the Monastery of St. Calixtus.

The Bible of Metz, presented to Charles the Bald by Count Vivien, Bibl. Nat., Paris, A. F., No. 1.

The Gospels of Metz, Bibl. Nat., Paris.

The Sacramentarium of Metz, Bibl. Nat., Paris.

The Hours of Charles the Bald, Bibl. Nat., Paris.

The Bible of St. Denys, written for Charles the Bald, Bibl. Nat., Paris, No. 2. a fragment of which is in B. M., Harl. 7551.*

The Psalter of Charles the Bald, Bibl. Nat., Paris, No. 1152, golden initials and purple vellum.

The Gospels of Louis le Debonnaire, Bibl. Nat., Paris.

The Gospels of Lotharius, son of Charlemagne, Bibl. Nat., Paris, A. F. 266.

The Gospels of Francis II., Bibl. Nat., Paris.

The Bible of Alcuin, B. M., Add. 10,546.

The Bible in the library of the Cathedral at Bamberg, a fac-simile of the Alcuin Bible, in the British Museum.

The Sacramentarium of Drogon, Son of Charlemagne, Bibl. Nat., Paris.

The Gospels of Ebon, Archbishop of Rheims, in the library of Epernay.

The small Psalter of King Athelstan, B. M., MS. Cotton, Galba, A. 18.

The Coronation Oath-book of King Athelstan, B. M., Cotton., Tiberius, A. 2.
These last two resemble the modifications of the Charlemagne style found in Anglo-Saxon MS.*

The Purple Psalter of Mr. Douce, in the Bodl. Libr., Oxford.

The Sacramentarium of Rheims, No. 320.

Other MSS. of the Eighth to the Eleventh Century, of various styles.

The Terence of the Vatican Library, ninth century, No. 3868.

The Terence in Bibl. Nat., Paris, No. 7899.

Cicero's Translation of Aratus, ninth century; British Museum, Harl. No. 617 (Cottley in archæologia).

The Great Bible of St. Martial of Limoges, tenth century, Bibl. Nat., Paris, A. L. No. 5. (Bastard).

Pontificale of the Library of Minerva at Rome (D'Agincourt).

Two Copies of the Gospels, eleventh century, B. M., Harl. MS., 2820 and 2821.

The Sacramentarium of Gelloni; Bibl., Nationale, Paris, eighth century.

Anglo-Saxon MS. of the Tenth and Eleventh Centuries, in the peculiar style supposed to be the "Opus Anglicum."

The Gospels of King Canute, B. M., Royal MS. 1 D. ix.

The Benedictional of St. Æthelwold, in the library of the Duke of Devonshire.

The two Benedictionals in the Public Library of Rouen.

Latin Psalters, B. M., Arundel, Nos. 60 and 155. No. 60 is a curious modification of the Canute style, the ornaments only spraying outward.

Psalter, B. M., Cotton., Tiberius, C. 6.

The Gospels in the library of Trinity College, Cambridge.

The Gospels in the library at Holkham.

MS. in B. M., Arundel 83.

Sacramentarium in Bibl. Nat., Paris, No. 987.

The Metrical Paraphrase of Caedmon, Bodl. Libr., Junius, No. 11.

The Anglo-Saxon Heptateuch, B. M., MS. Cott. Claud., B. iv.

Aldhelm, Treatise on Virginity in the Library of the Archbishop of Canterbury, Lambeth.

Gospels in B. M., Butler, 11,850, a curious variety of this style.

Lombardic MSS. from the Ninth or Tenth to the Thirteenth Century.

Bodl. MS. No. 176. Lombardic Gospels, tenth century.

Corp. Christ. Coll., Camb. MS. of Origen's Homilies on St. Luke, Lombardic, ninth century.

Bibl. du Roi at Paris, St. Augustine on the Pentateuch, Lombardic.

Vatican, No. 1671, Virgil, in Lombardic character, twelfth century.

Bodl. Libr., Bibl. Can. 61, Lessons from the Gospels, eleventh or twelfth century, Lombardic.

Bodl. Libr. Psalter (Douce MS. cxxvii.), ninth century, fine.

In the Monastery of La Cava, near Naples, the following seven Lombardic MSS., viz.:

    A Bible in elegant Lombardic, ninth century.

    The Treatise of Bede "De Temporibus," tenth century.

    Code of Lombardic Laws, eleventh century.

    Homilies and Hymns, twelfth century.

    Commentaries of Job, thirteenth century.

    The book "De Septem Sigillis," thirteenth century.

    The "Vitæ Patrum Cavensium," thirteenth or beginning of the fourteenth century.

Continental and Anglo-Norman MSS. of the Eleventh and Twelfth Century.

MS. of Countess Matilda, eleventh century, in the library of Sir T. Philips, described by Ottley in Archæologia, vol. xxiv.

Poems in honour of the Countess Matilda, Vatican Library, 4922.

Missals of St. Denis and of St. Maur, Bibl. Nat., Paris.

Harmon's Commentary of Ezekiel, Bibl. Nat., Paris.

The Psalter of Eadwine, in the library of Trin. Coll., Cambridge.

The Arnstein Bible, B. M., Harl., 2798 and 2799,* late twelfth century.

Lives of the Saints, B. M., Harl., 2800, 2801, and 2802, late twelfth century.

A MS. of the same period as the Arnstein Bibl. very fine letters, B. M., Harl., 3045.

The Worms Bible, B. M., Harl., 2803 and 2804, late twelfth century.

The Old Testament, B. M., MS. Reg. 1, C. 7.

The Life of St. Guthlac, B. M., Harl., Charters, Y. 6.

The Latin Psalter of M. Commarmond, with Byzantine paintings, and very rich gold capitals, now in the British Museum, Egerston MS. No. 1139 ; the covers are of exquisite and unique carving in ivory, twelfth century.

Lives of Saints, B. M., MS. Arundel, 91.

Latin Psalter, B. M., Arundel, No. 157.

Life of St. Edmund, with 32 miniatures, formerly in the Townley Library, now belonging to Mr. Holford.

Latin Bible, in the Bibl. Nat., Paris, t. 1, L. No. 8.

Latin Gospels, in the Bibl. Nat., Paris, A. F. 275 and 817, and 140, St. Germ. and S. L. 1118.

Other MSS. in Bibl. Nat., Paris, No. 818, 1049, 2058, 5058, and 5084.

The MS., No. 267, in the library of the Sorbonne, Paris.

Italian Historical Treatise, Vatican Library, 927.

Chronicles, in the Barberini Library at Rome, 3577.

B. M., French and Latin Psalter, Cot. Vit., 2 ix., eleventh century.

B. M., Bibl. Reg. 1, D. x., a fine copy of the Gospels, eleventh century.

The Commentary on the Revelations, in Visigothic letters, B. M., MSS. Add., 11,695.

The Visigothic Apocalypse, Bibl. Nat., Paris, S. L. 1076.

Bodleian Lib., Douce, ccxciii., a fine Psalter of the beginning of the twelfth century.

B. M., Bib. Reg., Psalterium et Litania, fine MSS. of the beginning of the twelfth century.

B. M., MS. 12, F. xiii., containing a bestiarium, &c. &c.

B. M., Bible Harleian, 2797.

A MS., B. M., Arundel, 490, fine initial letters.

Officia Sanctorum, Bodleian, 736.

A Psalter, in the Bodleian Library, Gough MSS., No. 194.

A small Psalter, in B. M., Lansdowne, 383.

A MS., in B. M., Butler, 11,847.

A Psalter, B. M., Harl., 2904.

Two vols. containing Maccabees and New Testament, B. M., Harl., 1526 and 1527.

A ditto, B. M., Harl., 5102.

A ditto, in B. M., Lansdowne, 431.

Latin Psalter, B. M., Cotton. MS., Nero, C. iv.

A Bible, B. M., with date (1148 A. D.), additional MSS., 14788-9-9.

MSS. of the Thirteenth Century.

Quinquepartite Psalter, in Bibl. Nat., Paris, 1132, Suppl. F.

Vriget de Solas, in Bibl. Nat., Paris, S. F., 11½.

A MS., in B. M., Royal 1, D. i.

Prayer-book of St. Louis, or rather of Queen Blanche, in the library of the Arsenal, Paris, No. 145, B. (Latin).

Hours of St. Louis, Bibl. Nat., Paris.*

Psalter of St. Louis, with 78 miniatures, in Bibl. Nat., Paris, presented by Louis XVIII.

Gospels of St. Martial, of Limoges in the collection of Count Bastard.

Psalter, in the library of — Holford, Esq.*

History of Troy, B. M., MS. Reg. 20, D. i.

Life of Edward the Confessor, Public Library, Cambridge, Ee. 3, 59, in Anglo-Norman verse.

The Bestiarium, in the Ashmolean Museum, Oxford.

The Apocalypse, in the library of Trinity College, Cambridge.

Medical Treatise, B. M., MS. Sloane, 2435.

Roman du Roi Artus, Bibl. Nat., Paris, No. 6963, A. F. (dated 1276).

Roman du Saint Graal, Bibl. Nat., Paris, No. 6769

Bible, No. 1, of the Sorbonne Library, Paris.

Decretals of Gratian, executed in Germany, Bibl. Nat., Paris, 3884.

Lectionarium, in Bibl. Nat., Paris, No. 2287.

Chronicle of the Monastery of Cluny, Vatican Library, 3839.

MS. of Sacred and Profane History, with 86 miniatures, Vatican Library, 5895.

Tragedies of Seneca, Vatican Library, 355.

Treatise on Hawking, written for the Emperor Frederick II., Vatican Library.

B. M., Bibl. Reg. 20, D. vi., a very fine MS.

A fine Psalter, New College, Oxford, 322, peculiar in style.

A fine Psalter, All-Souls College, Oxford, V. V. 2.

An exquisite MS., of the highest character of true Parisian art, of the period, (end of thirteenth century) B. M., Additional, 17,341.

MSS. of the Fourteenth Century.

Petrarch's copy of Virgil, illuminated by Simone, in the Ambrosian Library at Milan.

A MS., B. M., Royal 893.

Breviary of Queen Mary, B. M., MS. Reg. 2, B. 7.

Psalter, B. M., Arundel, No. 82.

A MS., B. M., Roy. 6, E. ix.

The Louterell Psalter in the possession of Mr. Weld.

Latin Psalter of Lord Braybrooke.

Latin Poems, B. M., MS. Reg. 6, E. ix.

Latin Graduale, B. M., Lansdowne MS. 463.

Les Gestes des Roys de France, B. M., MS. Reg.

Life of St. Denis, Bibl. Nat., Paris, 7953, 7954, 7955.

Life of St. Louis, Bibl. Nat. de Paris, 10,309.

The Merveilles du Monde, Bibl. Nat., Paris, 7892.—A fine MS. in the same style as the B. M., Harl. 4947. Another of the same school, is in the B. M., Egerton, 1076; both very late fourteenth or beginning of fifteenth century.

Chronique Universelle, Bibl. Nat., Paris, 6890.

The Liber Regalis of Westminster Abbey.

The Bible of the Emperor Winceslaus, at Vienna, in 6 fol. vols.

Italian History of the Old Testament, formerly belonging to the Duke of Sussex, now in Brit. Mus.

Psalter, Doucean Coll., in Bodl. Library.

The MSS. in Bibl. Nat., Paris, numbered 6701, 7031, 8395.

History of the Order of St. Esprit, Bibl. Nat., Paris, F. la Vall., No. 36.

Prayer-Book of the Duke of Anjou, Bibl. Nat., Paris, F. la Vall., 127.*

Translations of Boccacio, Bibl. Nat., Paris, 7091, and S. F. 540-8.

Bibl. Douce, lxii, lxxx, two fine MSS. of the end of fourteenth century; illustrating the games and sports of this country.

Harl. MS. 2435. L'Image du Monde, and a curious Medical Work in French, beginning of the fourteenth century, long finials to letters, a fine and curious MS.

Bibl. Reg. 6, E ix. Book of Poems belonging to Robert of Anjou, early in fourteenth century, curious Byzantine art.

Harl. MS. 2897. Latter half of fourteenth century, with curious finials to letters.

Harl. MS. 1319, Metrical Hist. of Richard II., a curious and valuable MS. for costume, written about the end of fourteenth century.

Fine Psalter in B. M., Arundel, 83, one of the most remarkable MSS. of the period.

Bodl. Libr., Bibl. Bodl., No. 264, a fine and valuable copy of the "Romance of Alexander," written in the year 1338, profusely illustrated.

Harl. MS. 2,897, a Beautiful Lectionary, fourteenth century.

Cotton. MS. Tib. B. viii., a very fine MS., commonly called "Charles Fifth's Coronation Book," profusely illustrated.

Bibl. Reg. 2 A. v., a curious MS. for grotesques and finials of birds' heads, &c., eight illustrations, and six letters on backgrounds of burnished gold.

Bibl. Reg. 2, B. iii., Psalterium et Litania, a beautiful MS., seven fine and curious illustrations on backgrounds of burnished gold.

Bibl. Reg. 2, A. xxii., Psalterium et Hymni, another fine MS., with illustrations on burnished gold backgrounds.

Egerton MS. 745, fine MS. of fourteenth century, seventy-six illustrations, exceedingly curious.

Bibl. Reg. 10, E. iv., Liber Decretalium, formerly belonging to the House of St. Bartholemew's in Smithfield; a most curious MS. for grotesques, in which the lower margin abounds, but the drawings are rudely executed.

The fine German Apocalypse lately in the library of the Duke of Sussex.

Bibl. Reg. 20, D. i., "Hist. Universelle jusqu à Jesu Crist," fine for armour, very similar to the Meliadus in Addit. MSS, B. M.

Bibl. Reg. xv. D. ii. Lucidarium, early fourteenth century, a very fine specimen of a MS. of this period both for letters and illustrations.

Bibl. Reg. 16, G. vi., "Gestes des Roys de France," 417 illustrations, curious and valuable; a very fine MS., early fourteenth century.

Harl. MS. 7028, fine fragment of a Lectionarium belonging to Salisbury Cathedral, end of fourteenth century.*

Bibl. Reg. 19, D. ii., "La Bible Historiaux," fourteenth century; known as The POICTIERS BIBLE, taken from the tent of King John of France at the battle of Poictiers.

Bibl. Reg. 19, B. xv., "Exposition d'Apocalypse du S. Jehan," fine MS., fourteenth century.

Bibl. Reg. 20, B. vi., the Amours of Charles the VI. of France, and Richard II. of England.

Romance of Meliadus, B. M., Additional, 12,228, interesting MS.

A Missal B. M., Egerton, 945.

A fine MS. B. M., 2908.

A fine MS. in Fitzwilliam Museum, Cambridge, No. 60.

Wickliff's Bible, end of the fourteenth century, Public Library, Cambridge; a late modification of the tenth century style, similar to the Salisbury Lectionarium in B. M.

MSS. Fitzwilliam Museum, Cambridge, 130, 63, 136.

A fine MS. in Trinity College, Cambridge, B. 11, 5.

Those MSS. marked Bibl. Reg. are of the Royal Library, in the British Museum.

Italian MSS. of the Fourteenth and Fifteenth Centuries.

Tragedies of Seneca in the Vatican Library, No. 1585 and 356.

Orations of Demosthenes, B. M.*

Decretals, &c., Vatican Library MSS., No. 1389, 3747, 2639, 501, 2094, 214.

Pliny, Bodleian Library, in Italian Arabesque, similar to our plate from the Roman History of the Arsenal.

The Latin MSS. in Bibl. Nat., Paris, No. 5888, 6246, 5041, D. and Fr. 994.

Books of Prayers executed for Hercule D'Este, in collection of Baron D'Hervey.

F

A MS. Petrarch, B. M., 3577.

Triumphs of Petrarch, translated, Bibl. Nat., Paris, No. 6877 and 7079.

Bible of Pope Clement VII., Bibl. Nat., Latin 18.*

Missal of the same Pope, in the same library.

Missal of Pope Paul V., Bibl. Nat., Paris.

Dante's Inferno, sent by King Edward IV. of England to the Duke of Urbino, illustrated by D'Agincourt, plate 77.

Bible of the Duke of Urbino, executed in 1473, in the Vatican Library.

Breviary of Matthias Corvinus V. of Hungary, Vatican Library, No. 112.

Justinian, in All-Souls, Oxford, W. 2, similar, but inferior in style to the Pope Clement Bible. Small specimens of the style exhibited in the superb Bible of Pope Clement VII. will be found in the two following MSS. in the British Museum, but both poor; additional MS., 11,999, and additional MS., 15,286, in the latter the ornaments are partially mixed with another style; there is also a large but very poor and coarse specimen in the additional MS., 15,287.

Harl. MS. 4965, Eusebius de Evangelica Præparatione, fine Italian MS., arabesque borders, with medallions, close of the fifteenth century.

Fragments of a Devotional MS., Italian, late in the possession of W. T. Ottley, Esq., close of the fifteenth century.

A fine printed Italian work in the possession of P. A. Hanrott, Esq., containing the " Deeds of Francis Sforza, Duke of Milan," A. D. 1490.

Harl. MSS. 3109, 4902, Italian MSS., middle of the fifteenth century.

The printed Pliny in the Douce col. (Bodlean Lib.), printed at Venice, in 1476, rich illuminations by hand, in the Italian style of the period.

The printed Life of Sforza, Duke of Milan, in the Grenville collection in the B. M., exquisitely illuminated by Girolamo dai libri.

MS. of the Fifteenth Century.

Prayer-book of Henry VI., B. M., MS. Cott. Domitian xvii.

A Missal in B. M., Harl. 2900.

Lydgate's Life of St. Edmond, B. M., MS., Harl. 2278.*

Poems of Christian de Pisan, B. M., MS., Harl. 4431.

A MS. with fine miniatures, B. M., Harl. 1892.

A MS. called the " Psalter of Queen Mary," B. M., Reg. 2, B. vii.

The Bedford Missal, in the collection of the Rev. J. Tobin, of Liscard, near Liverpool.

Psalter, and two fragments of a Missal in the possession of Mr. Owen Jones.*

Latin hours, B. M., MS., Harl. 2952, 2936, 3109.

French translation of Valerius Maximus, B. M., MS., Harl. 4374, 5.

Valerius Maximus, Bibl. Nat., Paris, F. 2794.

The great Chronicles of Froissart, B. M., MS., Harl. 4379, 4380.

Comedies of Terence, in the library of the Arsenal of Paris.*

Pier le Mangeur's French Biblical History, belonging to John King of France, B. M.

The small Hours of the Duke de Berry, Bibl. Nat.

The great Hours of the Duke de Berry, Bibl. Nat., Paris.*

The French Biblical History of the Duke de Berry, B. M., Harl. MS. 4381, 4382.

French Version of the Bible, B. M., MS., Reg. 15, D. iii.

Josephus's History of the Jews, Bibl. Nat., Paris, 6891.

The great Chronicles of England, probably a copy of la Chronique de Wavrin, executed for King Edward IV., B. M., MS., Reg. 14, E. iv.*

La Chronique de Wavrins Sgr. de Forestel, of the same period as the preceding, Bibl. Nat., Paris.

Missal of King René, Bibl. Nat., Paris, No. 547.

Psalter of René of Anjou, in the Library of the Arsenal, Paris.

Hours of René of Anjou, Bibl. Nat.

Treatise on Tournaments, illuminated by King René, Bibl. Nat., A. F. 8352.

The Romances presented by the Earl of Shrewsbury to Margaret of Anjou, B. M., MS., Roy. 15, E 6.

The Prayer-book of Mary of Burgundy, in the collection of the Rev. J. Tobin.

Cotton. MS., Augustus, A. v., Thesaurus Historiarum, fine MS., with 54 large illustrations, late in the fifteenth century.

Cotton. MS., Nero, D. vii., a curious book, being a Catalogue of the Benefactors to St. Alban's Monastery, upwards of 200 rude but curious paintings.

Cotton MS., Nero, E. ii., Les Chroniques de St. Denis, a fine MS., formerly unserviceable, on account of its having been damaged by fire, but now finely restored, 2 vols. folio, 88 fine illustrations.

Bibl. Reg., I. E. ix., a fine MS. of a large size, a copy of the entire Bible in Latin, 152 illustrated letters, with figures and fine ornamented margin, fifteenth century.

Bibl. Reg. 2, B. 15, a Breviary formerly belonging to Queen Mary, the art inferior Flemish, fifteenth century.*

Bibl. Reg. 14, E. iv., Les Chroniques D'Angleterre, fine copy of this class of MS., 26 large illuminations, fifteenth century.

Bibl. Reg. 18, D. vii., fine MS. of Boccace des Cas des nobles Hommes et Femmes, early in the fifteenth century, fine borders and illustrations.

Bibl. Reg. 19, E. v., Romuleon ou des faits des Romains, a fine MS., late in the fifteenth century.

Bibl. Reg. 20, B. xx., L'Historie d'Alexandre le Grand, early in the fifteenth century, fine MS. copiously illustrated

Cotton. MS., E. iv. 55, fine outline drawings, by John Rous, illustrating the Life of the Earl of Warwick, fifteenth century.

Bibl. Reg. 15, D. i., fine copy of the Historia Scolastica, fifteenth century.

Bibl. Reg. 18, E. ii., a fine copy of Froissart's Chronicles, latter half of the fifteenth century.

Bibl. Reg. 18, D. ii., Lydgate's Story of Thebes, with other Miscellaneous Poems, a fine and curious MS., latter part of the fifteenth century.

Bibl. Reg. 19, C. viii., L'Imaginacion de vraye Noblesse, a manuscript with a few illustrations; the art similar to the famous Rom. de la Rose.

Prayer-book of Mary of Burgundy, in the library of the Rev. J. Tobin, of Liscard, near Liverpool.

Breviary of Queen Isabella of Spain in the library of the Rev. J. Tobin.

B. M., Bibl. Reg. 20, C. iii., Boccace Book of Noble Women, in French, fifteenth century, late, borders like the Rom. de la Rose.

B. M., Bibl Reg. 20, C. vii., Hist. des Rois de France, early in the fifteenth century.

B. M. Bibl., Reg. 17, E. vii., early in the fifteenth century, fine MS., 88 small and curious illustrations by French artists.

B. M., Bibl. Reg. 15, D. iii., La Bible Historiaux, fine and beautiful MS., 3 large and 105 small illustrations, with a profusion of beautiful borders, and initial letters, early in the fifteenth century.

B. M., Harl. MS. 6199, Heraldic Art, Order of the Golden Fleece, a beautiful MS. for Arms, with a few portraits, close of the fifteenth century.

Bibl. Douce xi., Psalterium, by Pietro Perugino, very beautiful, fifteenth century.

Bibl. Douce x., Horæ, with beautiful paintings, fifteenth century, Bodleian Library, Oxford.

Bibl. Douce xx., Horæ, fifteenth century,   do.,   do.

Bibl. Douce xciii., Horæ et Officia, fifteenth century, do.,   do.

Bibl. Douce cccxi., Horæ et Officia, fifteenth century, do.,   do.

Missal, B. M., Harl. 2896, very exquisite miniatures.

Le Remedes de l'une et de l'autre fortune, MS. in Bibl. Nat., Paris, very large paintings.

Harl. 2897, exquisitely illuminated MS., in the style of the " Hours" of Henry VI.

Harl. 2936, Horæ, Flemish art, middle of the fifteenth century.

A Breviary Bibl. Nat., Lavall, 82, exquisite MS., date 1434.

Fine MSS. of the Fifteenth Century, in the style of Mr. Owen Jones's Psalter, figured in this work.

A MS. Bodl. Laud., 164.

A MS., Fitzwilliam Museum, Cambridge, 565.

A MS., in Trinity College, Cambridge, B. 11, 12, or B. H. 12.

A MS., in B. M., Royal 2 A., xviii.

A Breviary, B. M., Bib. Reg. 2 B. 1, also mentioned in general list of MSS. of the fifteenth century.*

Italian MSS. of the Fifteenth Century, with borders or letters in the peculiar style of ornament formed of white interlacing branches.

B. M., Harl. MS., 2593.

B. M., Harl. MS., 2730, a MS. Juvenal.*

B. M., Harl. MS., 3293.

B. M., Harl. MS., 4960, more foliage than usual, and on a gold ground.

B. M., a MS. Petrarch, Harl., 3517.

B. M., a MS. Livy, Harl., 3694, portions of the manuscript in another style.

B. M., a MS. Plato, Harl., 3481, very fine letters and marginal brackets.

B. M., a MS., King's, 18.

B. M., Additional MS., 15,270.

B. M., ditto ditto, 14,783.

A MS., with the branch-work richly coloured, B. M., Burney, 175,* date, 1475.

A MS., with borders similar to the last, B. M., additional 14,817.

A fine Virgil in the Library of P. A. Hanrott, Esq., middle of the fifteenth century, Italian, interlaced borders.

Italian MSS. with borders formed of richly-coloured cables substituted for the branch-work (a rare style).

B. M., Burney, 292, some branch-work borders mixed with the cable letters.

The magnificent MSS. in the Bodleian Library, Canonici Ital., 85.

The MS. Virgil, in the British Museum, additional 14,815.

The MS. Livy, in the British Museum, Harl., 2663.

In B. M., the Additional MS., 1479, initial in this style.

A MS., partially in this style, BM., Additional, 15,286.

MSS. of the end of the Fifteenth and the beginning of the Sixteenth Century, in Grisaille or Camé Gris.

The Life of St. Catherine, Bibl. Nat., Paris.

Dialogues of Francis I. and Cæsar, B. M., Harl., 6205.*

The "Triumphs" of Petrarch, illuminated by the same artist as the preceding MS., library of the Arsenal, Paris.

Les Chroniques de Pise, B. M., Bibl. Reg. 16, F. ii.

Livre d'ordre de Jesu Christ, B. M., Bibl. Reg. 20, B. iv.

L'Histoire Scholastique, Bibl. Reg. 15, D. i.

St. Augustine de la Cité de Dieu, B. M., Bibl. Reg. 14, D. i., fine specimen.

A fine MS., in B. M., Italian Art, Burney MS., 257.

A Virgil, B. M., Additional, 11,355.

A Quintus Curtius, French translation, made for Margaret of York, large borders and miniatures, B. M., Royal, D. 4.

A MS., in B. M., Lansdowne, 1179.

Miracles of the Virgin, Bodleian Library, Douce, ccclxxiv., a very fine MS.

The Prayer Book of Queen Mary, in the Bodleian Library.

MS., in B. M., Harl., 2952 and 2915.

B. M., Bibl. Reg. 15, D. iv., Les Faiz du grand Alexandre, a very tine MS., 18 large and 34 small illustrations, rudely drawn, cameo gris, with bold borders to correspond ; fifteenth century.

MSS. of the end of the Fifteenth and early part of the Sixteenth Century, of the Italian, French, Flemish, and German schools.

Missal of King Henry VII., in the library of the Duke of Devonshire.

Prayer-book of King Henry VII., B. M., MS. Reg. 2, D. 40.*

The Romance of the Rose, B. M., Harl. MS., 4425.

Hours of Anne of Brittany, Bibl. Nat., Paris.*

Book of Hours, belonging to Mr. Holford, same style as those of Anne of Brittany.

Latin Translation of Eusebius, B. M., MS. Harl., 4965.

Latin Breviary, B. M., MS. Reg. 2, B. 15.

English Translation of Vegetius, B. M., MS. Reg. 18, A. 12.

Poems of the Duke of Orleans, B. M., MS. 16, F. 2.

Hours of the Emperor Charles V., at Vienna.

The Sherborne Breviary, at Sion House.

The Lectionarium of Cardinal Wolsey, in the library of Christchurch College, Oxford.

Hours of Anne of France, Bibl. Nat., Paris.*

Missal in the library of the Arsenal, Paris.*

Missal, illuminated by Lucas Von Leyden, in the Soane Collection.

Missal, said to be illuminated by Hemling, B. M., 17,280.

Missal, executed by Girolamo dai Libri, for the Duchess of Urbino, in the Bodleian Library, Oxford.

Prayer-book of Mary de Medicis, in Douce Collection, Bodleian Library, Oxford.

Roman History, in the library of the Arsenal, Paris.*

The Prayer-book of Henry VIII., B. M., King's MS., No. 9

The Psalter of Henry VIII., B. M., MS. Reg. 2, A. 16.

The Victories of Charles V., executed by Giulio Clovio, in the Grenville Library, B. M.

The Vatican Dante, illuminated by Giulio Clovio.

The Epistles of St. Paul, illuminated by Giulio Clovio, in the Soane Library.*

Lives of the Dukes of Urbino, with miniatures, by Giulio Clovio, in the Vatican Library.

The magnificent MS., by Clovio, in the private Library of the King of Naples.

Latin Missal, by Clovio, in the collection of Mr. Holford.

The Strife of Fortune and Virtue, B. M., Royal 16, F. 4.

Prayer-book of King Sigismund III., sixteenth century, B. M., Additional MS.

A similar volume in Bodleian Library belonging to Bona Sforza, wife of King Sigismund III., Bibl. Douce, xl., A. D. 1527.

Another, described by Dibdin, belonging to the same personage, in the library at Landshut.

B. M., Harl. MS., 3469, The Splendor Solis, dated 1582 (Flemish).

B. M., Add. MS., The Hours belonging to the House of Du Croy.

B. M., Add. MS., Eleven leaves of the Portuguese Genealogy, early in the sixteenth century, (Flemish art). Each illumination is separately framed.

Bibl. Reg. 14, C. iii., Eusebii Chronicon, late in the fifteenth or early in the sixteenth century, fine MS., with curious Italian ornaments.

Ashm. MS., No. 1504, An Herbarium and Bestiarium, with several pages of grotesque letters, about A. D. 1500.

A fine Devotional MS. (Italian) in the possession of Mr. Ottley, close of the sixteenth century ; miscellaneous composition, medallions, &c., &c.

Prayer-book of Francis I., in the possession of the Rev. J. Tobin, of Liscard, near Liverpool.

Bibl. Douce, xiv., A fine Book of Hours by Girolamo da Libri, beginning of the sixteenth century, Bodleian Library, Oxford.

Bibl. Douce, xxix., another fine Book of Hours by Girolamo da Libri, beginning of the sixteenth century, Bodleian Library, Oxford.

Bibl. Douce, ix., Horæ, with beautiful paintings, A. D. 1507, Bodleian Library, Oxford.

MSS. of the Sixteenth and Seventeenth Centuries.

The Venetian Diploma, B. M.* Additional MS.

MS., B. M., Harl. MS., No. 3649.

Book of Hours belonging to Henry II. of France, Bibl. Nat., Paris, A. F. 1409, and S. L. 677.

Hours of Louis XIV., at the Royal Hotel du Invalides, Paris.

Prayer-Book of Louis XIV., Bibl. Nat., Paris.*

Prayer-Book of Madame de la Valliere, now in the possession of Mr. Tite.

Recueil des Rois de France, presented to Charles IX. of France, Bibl. Nat., Paris.

Prayer-Book of Marg. of Baden, painted by Brentel, Bibl. Nat., Paris, Sup. Cat., No. 705.

The Great Rouen Graduale, illuminated by D'Eaubonne, Public Library, Rouen.

A Missal in B. M., Harl. 2953.

A Missal in B. M., Butler, 11,865.

The Missal of Versailles (Sylvestre).

A Book of Hours, by Nicholas Jarry, Bibl. Nat., Sup. Fran., 2299.

A MS. of the eighteenth century, belonging to the Chapel of Versailles, now in Bibl. Nat., Paris.

A Choral Book, late in the possession of Mr. Ottley, executed between 1623 and 1644.

The MSS. marked Bibl. Reg. belong to the Royal Library, in the British Museum.

I have not myself examined the whole of the MSS. inserted in this list, and therefore cannot answer for the precise dates assigned to each, which are, however, those commonly received as correct.

The Illuminated Books of the Middle Ages

Longman & Co.
1849

A MS. OF THE SEVENTH CENTURY, KNOWN AS THE "DURHAM BOOK."

PRESERVED IN THE COTTONIAN LIBRARY IN THE BRITISH MUSEUM.

NY manuscripts of this style still exist in the great libraries of Europe. But the one above named, from which we have taken our present illustration, is unequalled in the intricacy and elaborate finish of its ornaments, except by the "Book of Kells," preserved in the library of Trinity College, Dublin. These earliest northern specimens of the art of illumination appear totally uninfluenced by any Roman ideas, and are evidently the productions of a semi-barbarous people, untutored in the higher branches of the arts of design; for which higher feeling we see substituted laborious and endless intricacy, produced by the most ingenious interweaving of lines—a principle which is always discoverable in the first artistic attempts of barbarous nations, between whose works, however distant the locality or the epoch, we invariably find a close resemblance in general effect. The remaining monuments of ancient Mexico, the most ancient (and even modern) Chinese works, the rude carvings of the South Sea barbarian, or the more finished productions of the semi-civilized Hindoo, all display this character— laborious intersection of lines in both angular and circular interlacings. It is the universal first step in decorative art.

The style appears to have arisen in this country among our British and Irish, rather than our Saxon ancestors; although such manuscripts are generally termed Anglo-Saxon. Pagan Rome, although exercising exclusive domination in Britain from the second to the beginning of the fifth century, appears to have influenced the native arts but little. The aborigines were reduced to the state of an inferior race, who continued to practice their own arts and customs in obscurity. It was not till after the fall of the empire, and the establishment of Rome as the great centre of Christianity, that she really influenced the arts and manners of Northern and Western Europe; and then, when her power became really a pervading influence, not through her legions, but through her missionaries, the copies of the Gospel executed in Britain were ornamented by the native converts, not in a style of art borrowed during the occupation of the island by the Romans, but by the rude national devices obscurely preserved among them, uninfluenced by the purely military domination of the falling Roman empire.

Christianity may be said not to have been established till the Saxon supremacy was complete; yet the style of art which the strictly Saxon race devoted to the decoration of sacred books, differed from that which was practised by the original British races, still remaining tolerably intact in Wales, to the north of Yorkshire, and especially in Ireland, from whence the congenial races of Wales and Northumberland received the results of a gradually progressing civilization, whose original character had not been adulterated by Roman invasion, or subsequent Saxon domination. This style of decoration, founded on the interweaving of lines, may be said to have attained its perfection in Ireland, and perhaps in part of Wales, about the end of the sixth century, and perhaps about a century after, (on the establishment of Christianity,) in Saxonised England; for the Irish monastery of Iona founded a colony at Lindisfarne, near Durham, about 634, where the manuscript from which our specimen is taken, was executed about the year 698.

About the ninth and tenth centuries a distinct Anglo-Saxon style began to develop itself, of which we shall hereafter give specimens. It was partly founded on the style of which we are now treating, and partly upon a Continental one, which arose from various circumstances to be discussed hereafter, and whose character consisted principally in adding *foliage* to the simply intersecting lines.

The style, of which our present specimen is a fine example, and which is formed by a composition of intersecting lines of various colours, enriched by interwoven creatures of the lizard tribe, is exhibited to us in its remaining monuments, in three or four successive periods of development.

The first period may be distinguished by the grotesque character of the pictures representing the Evangelists, or other human figures, which are of the rudest possible execution, very closely resembling Mexican remains; and also by the inferiority of the merely decorative portions, consisting of large letters, enriched with interlaced line-work, which are of much poorer design and execution than our specimen. This period is well represented by the psalter preserved in St. John's College, Cambridge, of which an example is given in Westwood's "Paleographia Sacra Pictoria." It may possibly be assigned to as early a period as the early part of the sixth century.

The second period is illustrated by the wonderful volume known as the "Book of Kells;" also described at some length in "Westwood's Paleographia," &c. In this work the figures partake still of the grotesque character of purely barbaric art; but the decorative letters and borderings, and other merely ornamental portions, are of a degree of richness, intricacy, and sharpness of execution, unequalled by any other work of the style, either of a preceding or succeeding period; and in one feature, that of interlaced letters formed of the human figure, it is unique.

The third period may be illustrated by the beautiful manuscript from which our specimen is taken, which marks a decided improvement in the figure pictures, which have a somewhat Byzantine character; and the merely decorative features, as may be seen in our specimen, though not equalling the "Book of Kells" in gorgeousness of colour, or in the profusion of enrichment we have alluded to, yet displays an advance in the direction of harmony, and a certain completeness of style, which always marks the more perfect development of any branch of art.

Fourthly, It may be remarked, that although another style sprang up about the ninth century, still the practice of this style continued to be exercised in parts of England, and in Ireland and Wales, so late as the eleventh, and even twelfth century; of which the Gospels of MacDurnan, in Lambeth Palace, of about the eighth century, and the Gospels of Ricemarchus, in Trinity College, Dublin, of the eleventh century, may be cited as examples; the latter a most beautiful specimen of the style, with some characteristics peculiarly its own.

After this short sketch of the style, and its leading features and progress, it remains to describe somewhat more minutely the beautiful manuscript from which our specimen is taken.

It is marked in the Cottonian library as Nero, D, 4. This wonderful manuscript, as shown by an entry at the end of the book, in a handwriting nearly coeval with the main part of the manuscript, was written by Eadfrith, Abbot of Lindisfarne, in honour of God and St. Cuthbert. It is also stated that the Monk Œthelwald executed the illuminations—facts most important, as fixing the execution of the volume between 698 and 721.* Many marvellous stories are related by subsequent chroniclers of Durham, respecting miracles, &c., &c., performed by this richly decorated volume. The first ornamental portion of the book contains the Eusebian canons, enclosed in separate arched compartments, as usual in books of this and much later periods; but the grandest pages are, as is generally the case, those at the commencement of the four Gospels—the genealogical portion of the Gospel of St. Matthew having a separate one; and another is placed at the commencement of the Epistle of St. Jerome. Our specimen is the commencement of the Gospel of St. John. The spare page opposite to the commencement of the Gospels is occupied by a large square filled with the most intricately wrought patterns of a similar style to those in the large letters in our specimen; and one, in particular, of these masses of ornament is so rich and various in its detail as almost to bid defiance to the skill of any modern imitation. There is also a picture of the Evangelist at the commencement of each Gospel, betraying a Byzantine origin of design, though no such influence is traceable in the pages without figures. These figures, though barbarous in design, are executed with extreme neatness and precision. The other pages in the book are without ornament, except in one portion, where a smaller kind of capital letter is occasionally employed; such as the one at the head of this description, a double letter, forming M and A.

It will easily be perceived that the three large letters in our specimen, are I N P; the first letters of "In principium erat verbum, &c., &c." It will be seen that there is an interlinear Saxon translation of the Latin, possibly of a somewhat more modern date than the rest of the manuscript.

* St. Cuthbert died 687. Eadfrith held the see from 698 to 721. Œthelwald afterwards became Abbot of Lindisfarne, and died 737.

THE superb manuscript from which the border enclosing this description and the three following specimens are taken, is a copy of the Gospels written entirely in golden letters; a luxurious mode of expressing the veneration in which the Gospels were held, not uncommon about this period.

The first specimen forms a frontispiece to the Gospel of St. Matthew; it is composed of a large and boldly drawn figure of St. Matthew. The words he appears to be inscribing in the book which he holds are, " Venite ad me omnes qui laborant et onerati estis, et ego reficiam vos"—" Come unto me ye that labour and are heavy laden, and I will give you rest;" the words that follow appear to be, " Domini Dominus, Deus Omnipotens." The evangelist is seated in a chair of very grand design, beneath an architectural canopy supported by painted columns, in the upper part of which the angel (the symbol of St. Matthew) appears displaying a scroll, bearing, in Latin, the inscription,—" The book of the generation of Jesus Christ, the son of Abraham, the son of David." The upper corners are filled by peacocks feeding from bronze cups, and the surrounding border is similar to that on the opposite page. The whole picture is painted with great freedom, having much of the best character of the last stage of Roman art.

The next specimen is the grand page beginning the Gospel of St. Matthew. At the top is the usual "Incipit evangelium secundum Matheum"—" Here beginneth the gospel according to Matthew;" and then the capital L and I, grouped together, commence the passage, " Liber generationis ihu xpi, filii Davidi, &c."—" The book of the generation of Jesus Christ, the son of David," the words Jesus Christ being abbreviated in the usual manner. The great decorated initials are formed in a style mingling the interweaving patterns of the early Gallican and Merovingian style (resembling our Irish and Hiberno-Saxon styles), with the Romano-Gallic style, which formed the basis of the marked style practised in the provinces around Aix-la-Chapelle about the ninth century, which might be termed the Charlemagne style, as it flourished during his reign, and that of his sons and grandsons, of which style, the so-called Alcuin Bible in the British Museum is a fair specimen, though not of the highest class, but which is interesting as an example that manuscripts were sometimes re-copied with all their ornaments and decorations with the most scrupulous exactness; a duplicate of this very Bible being preserved in the library of Bamberg, in every respect so precisely similar, that the most experienced connoisseur could not distinguish them apart. To return to our specimen; the whole text of the page is written in capitals on a coloured ground, divided into bars or stripes to receive the lines of writing, and surrounded with a border composed of a number of small portions of different patterns, about half of which are well known patterns belonging to Roman decorative art, and the others (those forming the corners) of barbaric interlaced work. The whole is surrounded by a band of gold, in which

is a very inferior device, intended to imitate diagonal rows of small pearls attached to a blue fillet which has a red pattern upon it. This page, taken as a whole, is one of the finest examples of decorative writing in existence—with extreme intricacy of detail there is a grand simplicity of general plan, which exhibits both nobleness and richness, and seems the very beau ideal of a style for ceremonial copies of the Scriptures. It is superior in grandeur to the Irish and Gallican styles, and superior in richness to the Charlemagne style, which succeeded it; which last appears to have been formed by abandoning most of the features of Gallican origin, and adopting a larger portion of the late Roman.

The third specimen is a page from the Eusebian Canons; it is headed as " Canon Secundus, in quo tres." These canons, as is well known, are appended to all copies of the Gospels from about the fifth to the thirteenth century. The columns of numerals are usually divided by decorative pillars enriched with compartments of different rich patterns; the pillars being connected at the top by arches, which are again enclosed by a larger arch spanning all the smaller ones, the space formed by which is filled up either by the title or a rich ornament; in the present instance, the smaller arches are each surmounted by the emblem of the evangelist to which the column of references belong. The whole design is in the same mixed but grand style as the two first specimens.

The framing to the present description is from one of the ordinary pages of the book, which is written in two columns, and every page is surrounded by a similar bordering, each differing in the detail of the patterns. The one selected, with the exception of the corner pattern, bears so completely the impress of late Roman art, that one might suppose it the copy of a panel from the walls of Pompeii; not only on account of the patterns but the distribution of the colours, especially the vermilion and black relieved with buff. The space between the columns is occupied in the original by references to parallel passages in the other evangelists.

The different styles of this and neighbouring periods, which are closely founded on late Roman art, may all be considered to have originated in France, Gaul being the most civilised and the most thoroughly Romanized of all the northern provinces of the empire.

The manuscript was formerly in the French library of St. Genevieve, and was purchased by Harley, Lord Oxford, in 1724, now forming part of the Harleian Collection in the British Museum. In the Bibliothèque Nationale of Paris there is now a manuscript of very similar character, which MM. Chompollion and Silvestre assign to the ninth century, as it was originally presented to the church of St. Medard of Soissons by Charles the Bald; and it is possible that the Museum manuscript may be of the same period, though there are many indications of its being the work of the preceding century, as stated in the Harleian catalogue.

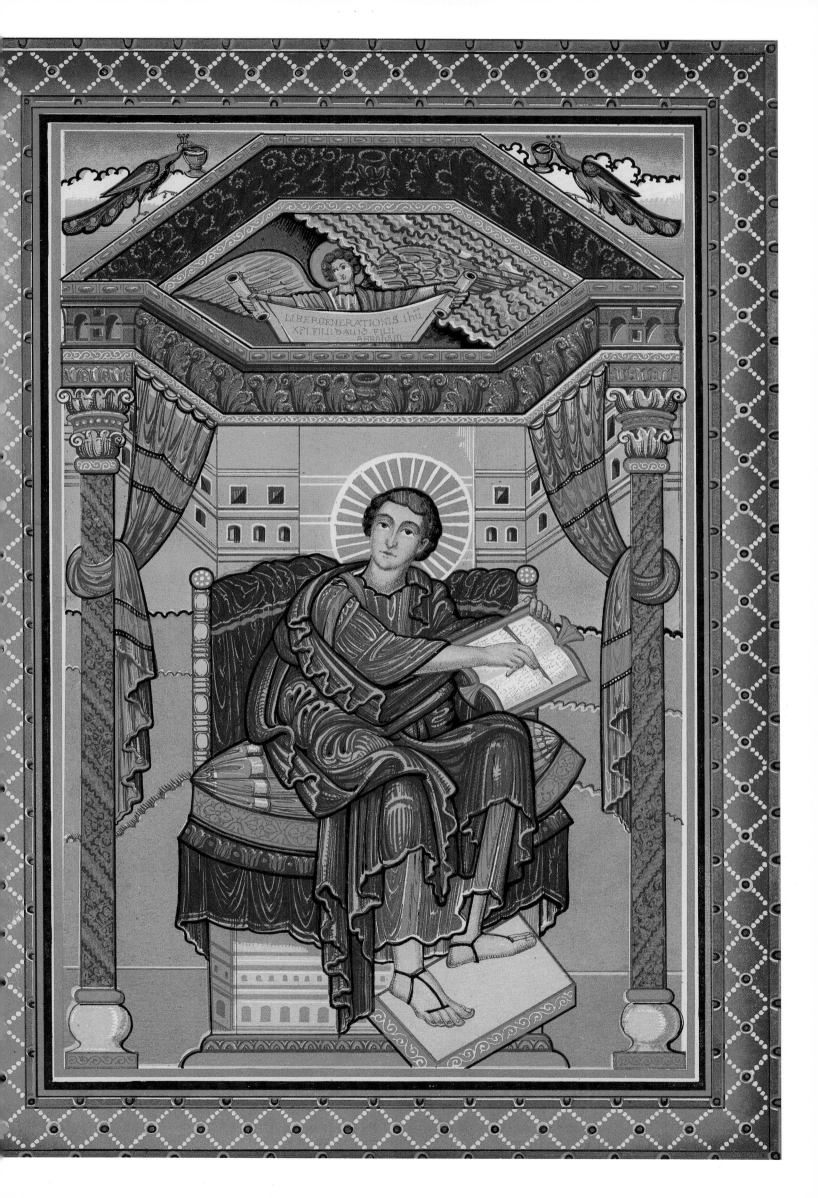

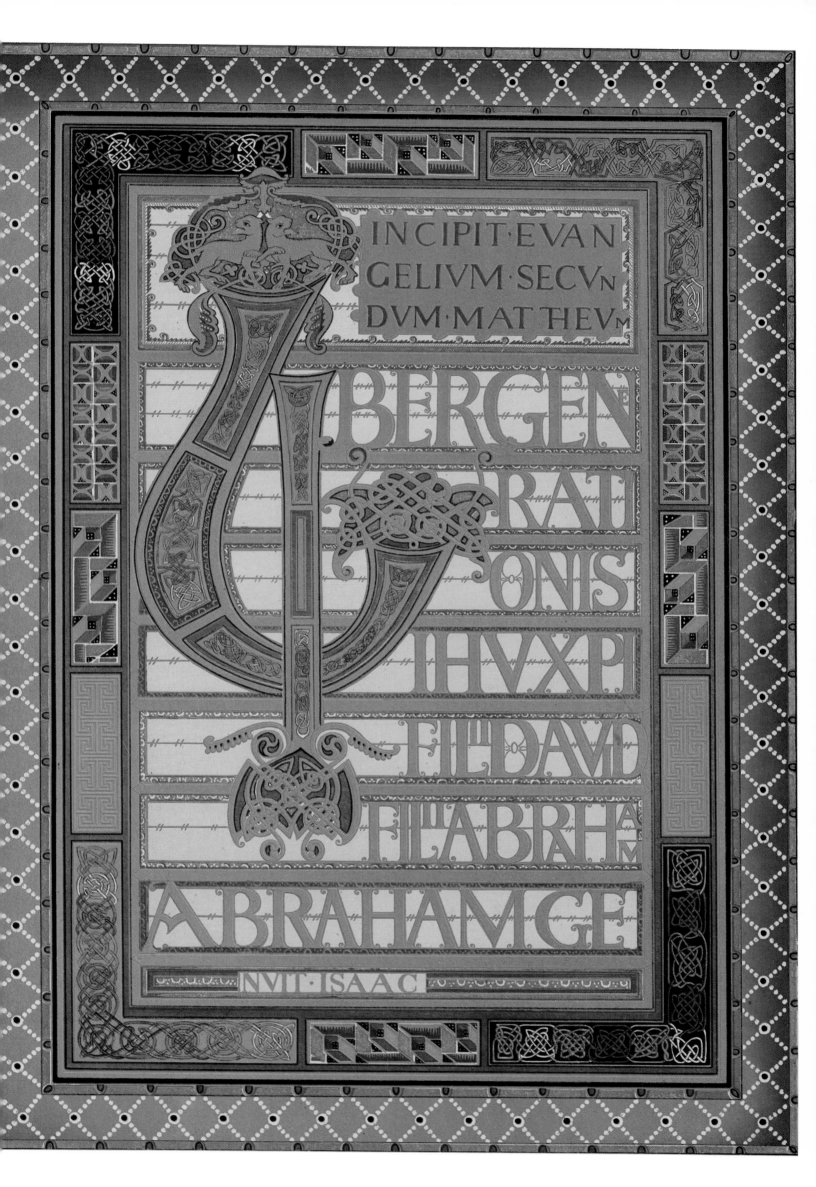

INCIPIT·EVAN
GELIVM·SECVn
DVM·MATHEVm

ꭤLBERGEN
eRATI
ONIS
IHVXPI
FILI·DAVID
FILII·ABRAHa m
ABRAHAMGE
NVIT·ISAAC

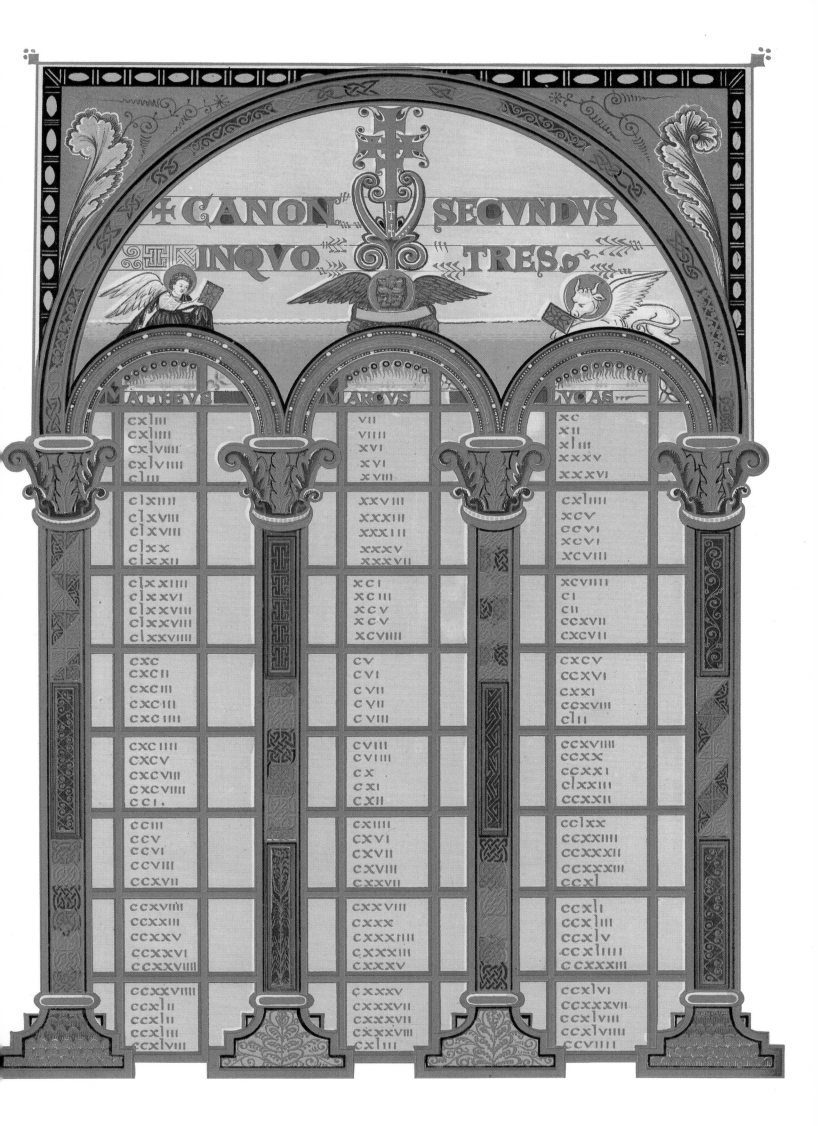

THE CORONATION BOOK OF THE ANGLO-SAXON KINGS OF ENGLAND.

A MS. FORMING PART OF THE COTTONIAN LIBRARY, IN THE BRITISH MUSEUM.

IN my sketch of the progress of the art of illumination at the beginning of this volume, I have spoken of the peculiar style which distinguished the period of Charlemagne, both in England and on the Continent, and still farther enlarged upon the subject in my description of the " Golden Gospels;" it is therefore unnecessary to repeat those remarks in this place. I shall, therefore, merely say a few words on the history of the interesting manuscript from which the accompanying specimens are taken. It is the copy of the gospels upon which our Anglo-Saxon kings took the coronation oath from the time of Athelstan; and from an inscription in the volume it would appear that the book was not written in England, but was a present received from Germany. The inscription stands " + Odda Rex," and " + Methild mater regis." The sister of Athelstan married Otho Emperor of Germany, from whom, and his mother Mathilda, it would appear that the book was a present to Athelstan. It is evidently a work of the ninth century, or very early in the tenth, and its paintings and ornaments possess all the peculiarities of works of that period.

It would appear that it was used at coronations as late as that of Henry VI.; an interpolated leaf belonging to a book known to have been executed for that king, appears to have been then inserted. After the Reformation, and the destruction of the monasteries and their libraries; such books were either destroyed or dispersed, on account of their idolatrous paintings, as they were termed; and this book, with many others, fell eventually into the hands of the great collector, Sir Robert Cotton, by whom it was produced at the coronation of Charles I., and in whose library it was subsequently much damaged by the great fire, which utterly destroyed many of the finest manuscripts of that invaluable collection. But of this circumstance, and other matters connected with the vicissitudes of this antique and venerable volume, Mr. Holmes, of the British Museum, has given an interesting and copious account in the " Gentleman's Magazine," for the year 1836.

The examples selected to illustrate the style of the illuminations of this manuscript, are a curious miniature of St. John, accompanied by his usual symbol, the Eagle, executed in the style of debased Roman art, which characterises the period. Opposite is the commencement of the Gospel according to this Evangelist, the large and finely-designed initial I of which forms a kind of border to the page, and is connected with the body of the writing by capitals of an intermediate size. The commencement of each Gospel is similarly decorated.

MORÆ VOLANS
ÆQUILÆ VERBO
PETIT ASTRA
IOHANNES

NPRIN
CIPIO

ERAT UERBUM ET UERBŪ
ERAT APUD Õ̃· ET Õ̃S
ERAT UERBUM· hoc ERAT
INPRINCIPIO APUD Õ̃
OMNIA PERIPSŪ FACTA SUN̄:
ET SINE IPSO FACTU ESC NIhIL
QUOD FACTUM ESC·
IN IPSO UITA ESC· ET UITA
ERAT LUX homINUM
ET LUX IN TENEBRIS LUCET
ET TENEBRÆ EAM NON
COMPREHENDERUNT
FUIT homo MISSUS AD Õ
CUI NOMEN ERAT IOhANNES
hIC UENIT IN TESTIMONIŪ
UT TESTIMONIŪ PERhIBER~

A FRAGMENT OF A BIBLE WRITTEN FOR CHARLES THE BALD,

NOW IN THE BRITISH MUSEUM.

THIS fragment is part of a magnificent Bible written for Charles the Bald, the grandson of Charlemagne; the other portion of which is in the Bibliothèque Nationale, Paris.

Charles the Bald was one of the greatest patrons of the art of illumination, and the number of books executed for him, and presented by him to various religious houses, must have been very great, or so many could not have been preserved to the present time: few of the great public libraries of France and part of Germany being without one or more manuscripts connected with the name of Charles the Bald. The Bibliothèque Nationale alone possesses several, among which the celebrated Bible presented to Charles the Bald by Vivien, Abbot of St. Denis, is perhaps the most magnificent and curious. It is enriched with many miniature pictures, and also with medallions, containing mythological subjects, designed with a classical feeling that is very extraordinary for the period. They are more like coarse Roman art of the period of the Antonines, than the Byzantine models from which alone we can suppose them derived. A prayer-book and a psalter written in letters of gold are also splendid monuments of the magnificence of Charles the Bald, possessed by the Bibliothèque Nationale. But the bible from which our specimen is taken is perhaps the most interesting of them all; from the curious blending of some of the most peculiar features of the Anglo-Hibernian style of the seventh, with the Continental style of the eighth and ninth centuries, in its principal initial letters. Indeed, the former style may almost be said to predominate. The upper ornament of the P in our specimen is entirely Anglo-Hibernian both in form and detail; and nearly the whole of its remaining details are also designed in a taste derived from the same source; whilst the general form of the letter is of the Continental style of the period, and the lower extremity, both in form and detail, is exclusively so. In short, it is such a singular mixture of styles as is rarely met with in manuscripts of early date.

Our specimen is the commencement of the Epistle to the Romans; the two lines at the top of the page are intended to read, "Incipit epistola ad Romanos"—(*here* begins the epistle to the Romans), the abbreviations being marked in the usual manner by a dash. It commences at the first verse (Paul, a servant of Jesus Christ, called to be an apostle, &c. &c.) It reads, "Paulus servus Jesu Christi vocatus apostolus." The A and U in Paulus are grouped into one character after a favourite fashion of the period. Jesu is written as usual with Greek characters; but the Greek H (eta) corresponding to the Roman E, is changed by the calligrapher into a Roman lower-case h, he having apparently understood the H as a common Roman character, by which alteration all meaning is lost. The S is omitted and the abbreviation marked in the usual manner.* Christi is also written in Greek characters, the X (chi) corresponding to the Roman ch; then the Greek sigma corresponding to the Roman S, or rather, a form representing it, and a small i within its folds—the RI and T being omitted, and an abbreviation marked. The VO in vocatus is singularly formed into one character, by making the V square at the bottom, by which means room is obtained for the O, which is made angular in a very arbitrary manner, merely, as it appears, to form a more picturesque composition. The C (singularly formed) and A follow in the same style, forming a line of writing, the whole effect of which is closely copied from Irish or Anglo-Irish manuscripts of an earlier period. The celebrated Book of Kells has a line very similar in character, but infinitely more rich both in composition and colouring.

Taken as a whole, this page is a very fine specimen of early calligraphy, the simple grandeur of which has been rarely surpassed in manuscripts of any period.

---

* The ingenuity of a later period has explained the I. H. S. still in use, and sometimes woven into a monograph—as signifying Iesus Hominum Salvator; whilst the Greek X (chi) of Christus has been considered a *cross*, and so used as a symbol of the name of Christ.

INCPT
EPTLA
ADROMNS

LVSSERVVS

TVSAPTLS

THE BENEDICTIONAL OF ST. ÆTHELWOLD,

IN THE POSSESSION OF THE DUKE OF DEVONSHIRE.

AND THE PSALTER, NUMBERED 83, IN THE ARUNDEL COLLECTION, IN THE BRITISH MUSEUM.

THE Benedictional* of St. Æthelwold is one of the finest remaining monuments of the arts of the tenth century; and its being undoubtedly the production of an English artist gives it an additional interest in this country. The singular and marked style, both of the composition and colouring of the ornaments of this manuscript, are peculiar to Anglo-Saxon works of the tenth century; and it is conjectured that it is this school of ornamental design which attained to so high a reputation among continental nations as to be sought in preference to the productions of their own countrymen, under the general name of " English work " (opus Anglicum). Some have thought that the earlier Anglo-Saxon, or rather *British*, style of the seventh and eighth centuries, as exhibited in the famous Durham book, was the celebrated " opus Anglicum ;" but that style of ornament was also practised, in variously modified manners, in several parts of the continent, the Lombardic illuminations of the same period bearing a very strong resemblance to it in general character. But of the marked Anglo-Saxon style of the tenth century, as exhibited in the Benedictional of St. Æthelwold, no authenticated continental examples occur, that I am aware of, which seems to favour the idea that the works of this class were the famous " opera Anglica," above referred to, for the style was not confined to the art of illumination only, the works of the architect and the jeweller of this period exhibiting sometimes the same style. The capitals of John's Church, Chester, and Steetly Church, Derbyshire, might be cited as examples,† and the crozier found in the tomb of the Archbishop Ataldus, who died in 933, and was buried in the cathedral of Sens. The Benedictional of St. Æthelwold, as appears by the metrical dedication, in letters of gold, was written for Æthelwold, bishop of Winchester, from 963 to 984, by the scribe Godeman, whom Mr. Gage considered also to be the illuminator.‡

Some of the miniatures are conceived in a very grand style, and if the powers of execution of the artist in this department had been equal to his intention, they would have been honourable to any period of art, the one representing Christ descending to judge the world, accompanied by a host of angels, bearing the instruments of his passion, may be especially distinguished. The ornaments are not open to the objection of inefficient knowledge of drawing or imperfect execution, and with their rich but chaste colouring and judiciously introduced masses of burnished gold, form a series of the most brilliantly illuminated pages that can be conceived. In the metrical dedication above mentioned the style of the work is alluded to ; it is stated that Æthelwold " commanded a certain monk subject to him to write the present book ; and ordered also to be made in it many *arches, elegantly decorated, and filled up with various ornamental pictures, expressed in divers beautiful colours and gold.*" Our specimen represents one of the subjects thus formed of " arches elegantly decorated, filled up with ornamental pictures." The pictures " filling up " being composed of a group of the confessors, which doubtless corresponded with an opposite page, now lost, containing another similar group, which perhaps completed the imperfect title " Confessoru⁻ " making it " *Chorus* Confessoru⁻" as in the two following pages, "Chorus Virginum." The costumes of the confessors are interesting, as early records of clerical costume, and exhibit the confessors as wearing the chasuble over the dalmatic and tunic, with the stole, which appears beneath. Above the chasuble hangs the superhumerale, joined with the rationale; and, over all, the pallium, spotted with crosses. Some of the miniatures are contained in a square framework of remarkable design, of which our second specimen, in a similar style, from the Arundel manuscript, in the British Museum, will convey a good idea, the place of the miniature alluded to being occupied, in the present instance, by a capital letter in the same feeling, a feature not to be found in the Æthelwold Benedictional.

The public library of Rouen possesses two manuscripts of this period, both English works, which found their way to that city during the union of Normandy with England ; the finest of them is known as the Benedictional of the Archbishop Robert. They are both evidently of the same school, and were most likely executed by the monks of Winchester.

Trinity College, Cambridge, possesses also a fine copy of the Gospels, in a closely similar style, and the British Museum, in addition to the Psalter, containing our second specimen, possesses the fine manuscript known as Gospels of Canute, the Cottonian Psalter, Tiberias C. 6 ; and in the Cottonian manuscript Vespasian A. VIII., a frontispiece, with surrounding ornaments in the same style ; and some other manuscripts, in which a similar description of framing to the square miniatures is found, but only in outline.

---

* The book contains forms of Episcopal Benedictions for one hundred and sixteen festivals.
† Westwood, Paleographia, &c.
‡ See Archeologia, vol. 24.

A BIBLE OF THE TWELFTH CENTURY,
NOW PRESERVED IN THE BRITISH MUSEUM.

NDER the head of illuminations of the twelfth century, we could not cite a finer example of the period than the specimen here selected. It is from a noble copy of the Bible, which contains some of the largest and most florid examples known of that peculiar style. In this manuscript, each book of the Old Testament commences with a large capital letter, similar to the U at the head of this description, generally with the figure of the historian or prophet artistically introduced in some part of the letter, and in some cases actually forming the letter itself; a peculiar feature not often found so strikingly treated in books of the period. The other, or secondary capitals, are merely in red outline, in the usual style of that epoch, but filled with party-coloured grounds, similar to those of the common Italian work of the early part of the fifteenth century. I allude to the style formed of white interlacing bands, which appears to have grown gradually out of the feeling of the capital letters of this period; some of which in this volume being very similar in the interlacings, and actually tinted in a yellow tone, like the white interlacings of the common Italian style of the fifteenth century.*

Our specimen is from the portion of the manuscript occupied by the New Testament, which is rather differently treated to the Old, each gospel commencing with a large ornamental compartment formed of the two or three first words, the first two or three letters of which are invariably of gigantic size, though varying in each case both in detail and general design. The page we have selected as the finest example is that containing the commencement of the Gospel of St. John, generally the one most elaborately decorated by the early illuminators. The words contained in the illumination are "In principio," after which the text continues as in the Latin vulgate. The heading of the chapter is written beneath, and reads, when translated, "Chapter the First. Christ, God from eternity, and man for a season—confirms the testimony of John the Baptist, and calls certain disciples." At a first glance the general effect of this illumination is not so effective as might be expected from its large size and the profusion of gold and rich colour employed. One seems to wish that the writing of the text, at all events that portion under the illumination, should be larger, and the small border enclosing the illumination have also enclosed the text below. But waiving these imperfections, or apparent imperfections, there is considerable art displayed in the composition; for instance, it might appear to a casual observer that the *I* should have been marked with the bold central black line so effectively introduced in the N. But the artist had another effect in view; he wished to make the I correspond with the smaller letters on the other side of the N, reserving the N itself as a *central* object; and the composition, regarded with this feeling, will appear very successful. Nevertheless, as a whole, it is less excellent than in parts, for the N, extracted and set apart, would be one of the finest specimens of a decorative letter of that or any other period. At the top of the N, St. John, accompanied by his associated emblem, the eagle, is represented in the act of writing his gospel, under the influence of inspiration, as expressed by a figure of Christ, which appears in a semicircular compartment above, holding out a book over the head of the Evangelist. It should be observed that in our copy the treatment of the faces is somewhat less marked and decisive than in the original, and the draperies scarcely so sharply and effectively indicated.

These volumes, as appears in a note in a handwriting of the period, belonged to the monks of St. Mary and Nicholas, of Arnstein, in the year 1464. And it is possible that they were originally executed for that religious house, as two other volumes of precisely the same style and period, as to the writing, contain a detailed life of the founder of that establishment. The value attached to these magnificent volumes may be inferred from the following singular anathema at the end of the first volume:—"Liber sancte Marie sanctique Nicolai in Arrinstein. Quem si quis abstulerit, morte moriatur, in sartagine coquatar, caducus morbus instet eum et febres, et rotatur et suspendatur. Amen;"—which may be translated, "The book of St. Mary and St. Nicholas, in Arrinstein; the which, if any one shall purloin it, may he die the death, may he be cooked upon a gridiron, may the falling sickness and fevers attack him, and may he be broken upon the wheel and hung."

Anathemas were not uncommon in valuable books, but generally more simple, such as, "If any one injure or take away this book, may he cursed, (anathema sit)."

These two volumes are numbered 2798 and 2799 in the Harleian manuscripts in the British Museum. The other volumes above alluded to, are numbered 2800, 2801, and 2802, and contain lives of the saints, &c. &c., with that of the founder of the monastery of Arnstein. Two other noble volumes of the same style and period, numbered 2803 and 2804, contain another copy of the vulgate. The style of the writing, that of the transition from the rounded character to the angular Gothic one, is so similar in all seven volumes as to appear written by the same hand, though that seems scarcely credible; it is, however, clear that they were all written towards the close of the twelfth or quite at the beginning of the thirteenth century. The last two volumes have an inscription in a comparatively modern hand, stating that they belong t the church of St. Mary, in the suburbs of the city of Worms, to which they possibly found their way, on the suppression of the convent of Arnstein.

* See description of the specimen of the white interlaced Italian style.

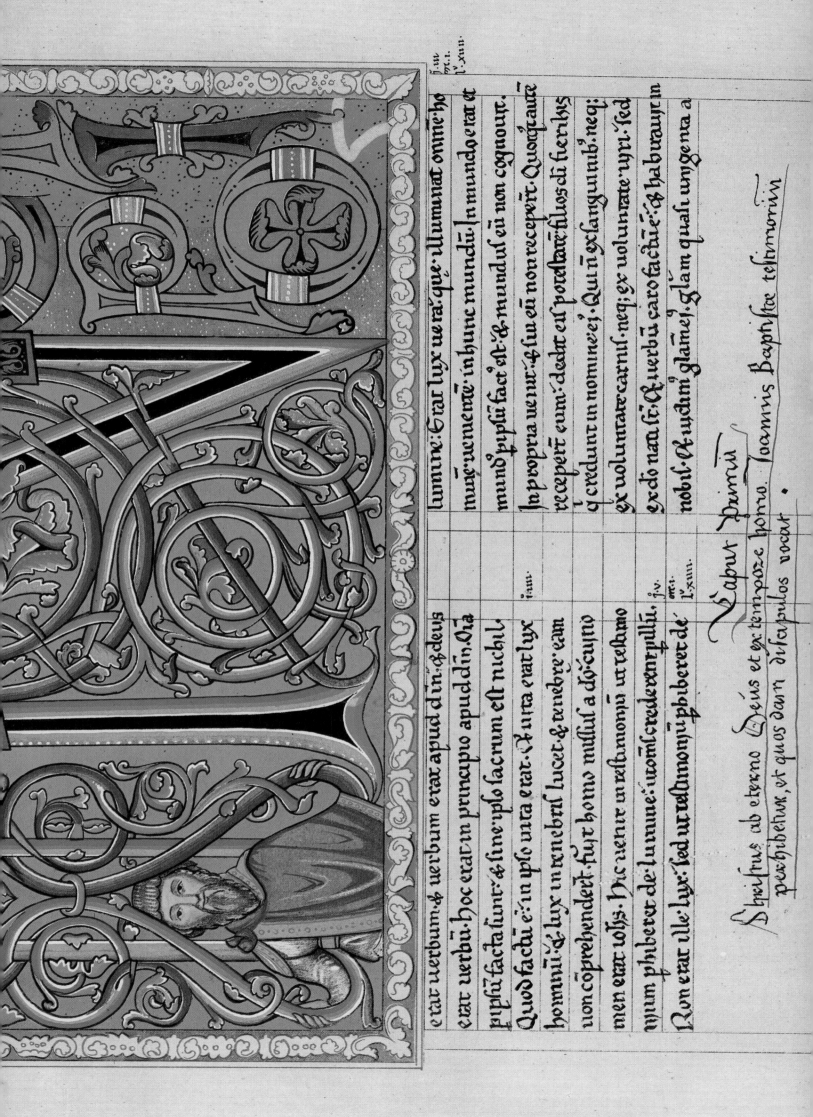

erat verbum. & verbum erat apud dm̄: & deus
erat verbū. Hoc erat in principio apud dm̄. Oīa
p ipm̄ facta sunt: & sine ipso factum est nichil.
Quod factū e: in ipso uita erat. & uita erat lux
hominū: & lux in tenebris lucet. & tenebre eam
non comprehendet. fuit homo missus a dō: cui no
men erat iohis. Hic uenit in testimoniū: ut testimo
niū phiberet de lumine: ut om̄s crederent p illū.
Non erat ille lux: sed ut testimoniū phiberet dē

lumine: Erat lux uera: que illuminat omne ho
mine ueniente in hunc mundū. In mundo erat et
mundus p ipsū factus est: & mundus eū non cognouit.
In propria uenit: & sui eū non recepit. Quotquot aute
receperūt eum: dedit eis potestate filios dei fieri hys
q credunt in nomine ei. Qui nō ex sanguinib: neq;
ex uoluntate carnis: neq; ex uoluntate uiri: sed
ex dō nati sūt. & uerbū caro factū e: & habitauit in
nobis. & uidim̄ glām ei. glām quasi unigenita a

Capur primū

Christus ab eterno Deus et ex tempore homo. Joannis Baptista testimoniū
perhibetur, et quos dari discipulos vocat.

THE "HOURS" OF ST. LOUIS,

PRESERVED IN THE BIBLIOTHEQUE DU ROI, PARIS.

THIS manuscript was executed about the middle of the thirteenth century, perhaps about 1250; but it does not present the ordinary features of ornament of the period, which consisted generally of richly interlaced foliage work, in which were introduced various grotesque animals, &c., &c. The ornaments of this volume are, on the contrary, extremely simple in their style; the small borderings round the miniatures, and large letters, being evidently founded upon Byzantine models, which still preserved much of the style and simplicity of ancient art. The costumes and architecture displayed in the miniatures, are, however, those of Western Europe of the period, the architecture being of that epoch of the Gothic, known among the architects of this country as "early English."

We have deviated in this instance from our rule of giving an entire page of each manuscript; for the "Hours of St. Louis" form a large folio volume, the text of which is written in two columns, the only decorative features being, the comparatively small miniatures and capital letters. An entire page would, therefore, only have exhibited an enormous mass of text, only enlivened by the capital D and the small miniature which we have selected as examples, and which, on that account, we thought it much better to detach. The capital D commences the words "Dixit incipiens in," which are contained within the same square. In the upper compartment of the letter there is a kneeling figure (probably that of St. Louis) before one of the Deity, enclosed in the symbolic *vessica piscis*.

In the miniature, the subject to the right is the sacrifice of Isaac, which is very curious, as representing Abraham in the costume of a knight of the thirteenth century, completely clothed in the chain armour of the period.

In the library of the Arsenal, another book which belonged to St. Louis is still preserved: it is a very richly illuminated psalter, the decorations of which are somewhat more in the usual style of the period, and of which it is our intention to give a specimen in this work.

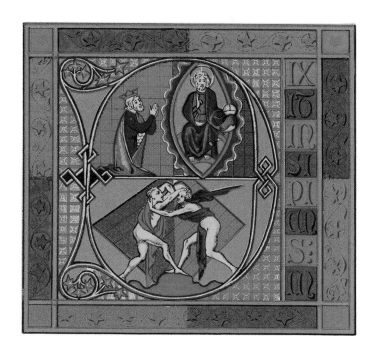

A PSALTER OF THE THIRTEENTH CENTURY.

PRESERVED IN THE BRITISH MUSEUM.

THE peculiar style of the thirteenth century, of which the present specimen is an example, is one founded upon that of the twelfth, as exhibited in our specimen from the Arnstein Bible. It is the same style carried into infinitely greater intricacy and slenderness of detail. In this style, generally, as in our example, the variously coloured ground is commonly abandoned for one entirely of gold; but many other variations of treatment occur during the course of the thirteenth century, which it would be impossible to treat of separately in the compass of this work. Yet it may be stated, that all the styles in the earlier portion of the century are characterised by a greater degree of finish, and greater delicacy in the smaller ornaments, than are exhibited in the preceding periods. Towards the close of the century, however, when the *angular* or *Gothic* feeling of ornament began to predominate, and the long-tailed letters to form themselves into marginal bars, the execution, as well as design, was sometimes exceedingly coarse, and the interlaced work as a feature was almost entirely abandoned. Indeed, the epoch of which our specimen is an example, may be considered the last stage of the interlaced style, as a leading principle of ornament.*

It first appeared in the Hibernian and Anglo-Hibernian manuscripts, was grafted upon the Charlemagne style of the eighth and ninth centuries, formed itself into a new and peculiarly complete style in the twelfth century, and worked itself out in infinitesimal ramifications in the thirteenth.

Many of the small figures introduced in the composition of this style of ornament are allusive to the subject, whilst others are merely decorative, as far as I have been able to discover. In our specimen, the two upper medallions represent—one, the ancient law, with its banner broken; the other, the new law, its banner erect, surmounted by the cross. Many other devices of a similar description were resorted to by the illuminators of this period to express the supremacy of the New Testament. Below, are two compartments containing figures of David; one playing on the harp, the other on a sort of viol. The connecting border is highly characteristic of the art of the period, and the different animals filling the interstices of the ornament are very carefully drawn. At the four angles, within the border, are the four symbols of the Evangelists—the angel, the eagle, the lion, and the bull. Among the small figures that appear in the convolutions of the great B, is that of David, in several different circumstances of his life.

Many of these figures are merely fanciful grotesques, such as the one holding a sort of dragon, which seizes the next figure as he is endeavouring to escape among the intricacies of the interweaving lines. Fanciful devices of similar character began to prevail at this period, especially towards the end of the century, when they were introduced profusely, and were not always of the most delicate nature. Our specimen contains the commencement of the first Psalm (Blessed is the man that walketh not in the council of the ungodly). The letters following the B make, with the great B, "BEAT VIR Q N ABIIT IN CŌSILᵇ IMPIOR," for " Beatus vir qui non abiit in consilio impiorum."

The I of qui is contained within the Q, the U being omitted; N with a mark of abbreviation stands for non; the N is omitted in consilio, the I and L are joined, and the final I O appear in smaller letters above the lower limb of the L. The Psalter has been considered the parent of the later Missal, and, from about the eleventh or twelfth century till the fourteenth, was almost as frequently produced in a richly illuminated form as the four Gospels. The first page is generally the only one illuminated in early manuscripts, but this in general very magnificently. A series of the magnificent B's enriching the first pages of Psalters from the tenth to the fourteenth century, would form a superb series, showing the progress of decorative art exercised upon one particular form in an interesting and striking manner, and proving that the same groundwork, or skeleton, is capable of being filled up with endless variety of design, even when of such marked character as in the instance of the letter B—which, at a glance, would appear to preclude the possibility of much variety of treatment.

---

* Excepting, of course, its reappearance in the beautiful Italian borders of the fifteenth century, elsewhere alluded to.

et in uia peccato2 nonstetit: et in cathedra pestilecie nsedit.

et in lege dni uolutas ei: et in lege ei meditabit die ac nocte.

Et erit tanqm lignu qd plantatu e secus decursus aqrum: qd fructu suu dabit intepo2e suo.   ie tre.

t folui ei non defluet: ce omia que cuq; faciet pspabuntur.

on sic impi n sic: ß tanqm puluis que proicit uentus afa

A PSALTER OF THE THIRTEENTH CENTURY,

IN THE POSSESSION OF R. S. HOLFORD, ESQ.

IFFERENT epochs of the art of illumination present widely different and distinct styles ; the most showy and best known, though perhaps the least pure and inventive in design, being that of the middle and end of the 15th century ; whilst the period perhaps the least generally known, that of the 13th century, may be considered as the most interesting and original : many of the best works of that period displaying an astonishing variety and profusion of invention. The MS., of which two pages form the opposite plate, may be ranked among the most elaborate and profusely ornamented of the fine books of that era ; every page being sufficient to make the fortune of a modern decorator, by the quaint and unexpected novelties of invention which it displays at every turn of its intricate design. One of the pages selected as specimens fully bears out these remarks : a pale blue dragon linked to a red fox-headed dragon, that seizes and combines itself with other intricate ornaments, (the tail of the former spreading itself into three compartments, each of which is a little picture, containing a cock, goats butting, and a monkey,) forms the upper part of the framework to the page ; the capital letters, joining on to interlaced fillets of different colours, form the principal side ; and the bottom is composed of a rich tail-piece, where a dragon and two knights charging form principal objects among the interlacing fillets and foliage. Even the stops contain a profusion of design : in one, a knight and a jester are in combat ; wit without armour being perhaps exhibited as a full match for brute strength cased in steel : below, a blue dragon vomits forth an amazon, armed with bow and arrow ; before whom up springs a naked imp, who insolently and somewhat indecorously proposes a target to the fair markswoman. The last stop displays a combat of dragons : a pink dragon has swallowed a blue dragon, whose sides, however, are unable to contain the angry tail of the swallowed opponent, which bursts through in its struggles, whilst the head and fore feet, not yet swallowed, attack a scarlet dragon, who swallows him down to the shoulders, but who finds his anterior portion as comfortless an inmate as the pink dragon had found the posterior extremity ; for the blue head bursts through the sides of the scarlet dragon, just as his tail had made a passage through the ribs of the pink one. In short, the *diableries* of modern French artists, even Henri Monnier himself, must cede the palm to the wild grotesque, or rather grottesque, of their rival of the 13th century. In some instances, the fancy of our illuminator has run riot too wildly, and become altogether indecorous : but these instances are comparatively rare, considering at once the great number of pages thus decorated, and more especially the gross and vitiated taste of the upper classes at that period.

It would seem, from the characteristic individuality given to some of the faces, that particular persons were indicated, or rather, caricatured ; especially a knight with a very singular nose, and a lady in the disguise of a knight, both of whom appear very frequently in these singular compositions. At the beginning of the volume is a miniature containing a family group, in which the principal female figure and the daughter wear crowns, the male figure and his son being without them. These circumstances may assist in the discovery of the name of the person — doubtless, some one of the highest rank — for whom this elaborate volume was executed. Some unusual words in that portion of the volume written in old French may also probably assist to determining in what part of France the book was executed, a point to which I shall return in the continuous sketch of the progress of the illuminator's art, which will accompany the last Number of this work.

The Psalms are preceded by a series of elaborate miniatures, representing the principal events in the life of David ; opposite to each of which, a page is dedicated to the description (in French) of the pictures. These descriptions are written in white letters, on alternate spaces of red and blue, separated by gold lines. Similar descriptions are found also opposite to large capital letters, of which several, similar to the D at the head of this page, occur in the volume. The description of the subject in our D, relative to the story of Abigail, is as follows : — " Dient comment ꝺꝺ envoie ✕ de ses cōpagnons por aucune vitaille a un riche homme de sen Linage qui faisait tondre ses brebis, & avait bele dame a feme & sage et avait nom Abigail, & li borgois Nabal il parla laidement a S. compagnons & dist kil ne leur donroit nient. li dame nen sent mot. il retornent a DD. il jure kil ne li laira rien de quā kes li Borgois a."— which may be literally rendered thus, — " representing how David sends some of his companions for provisions to a rich man of his lineage, who was shearing his sheep, and had a beautiful and discreet lady to wife, whose name was Abigail. And the burgher Nabal spoke rude words to these companions, and said he would give them nothing. The lady said not a word. They return to David (the lower compartment represents the return), who swears that he will leave to that burgher nothing of what he has."

The second page which I have taken from this MS. is one from the calendar, and is very remarkable : the ground being an entire mass of silver, varied with gold, blue, red, and green, gives it an air of barbaric magnificence of peculiar character ; and though the calendar itself contains no intricacies of design, it forms, perhaps on that account, a still more striking contrast to the elaborate tracery of the rest of the volume. The general features of the designs, in this volume, exhibit an interesting period of transition from the fine circular style of the 12th century, to the elegant and original pointed style of art which was soon so totally to supersede it. This incipient taste for pointed and attenuated forms is strikingly illustrated in the peculiar character of the long-tailed letters, not only of this MS., but of most others of the period.

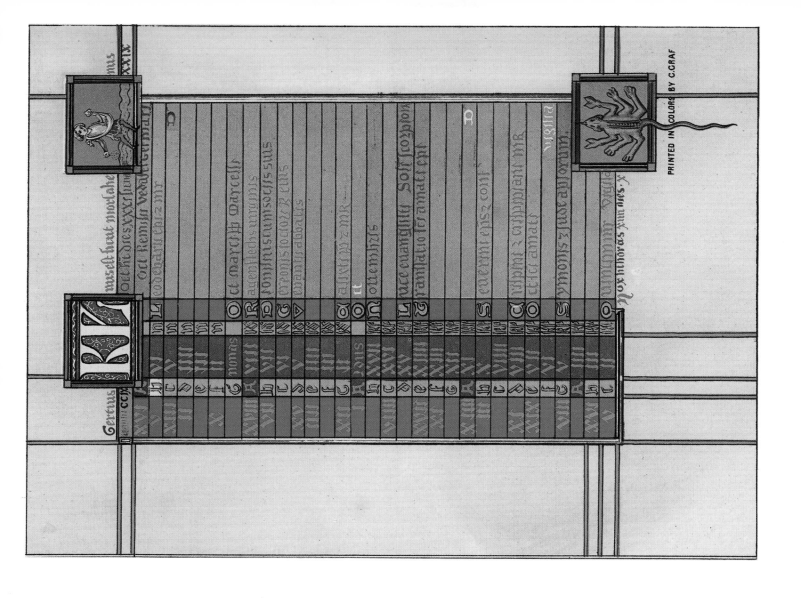

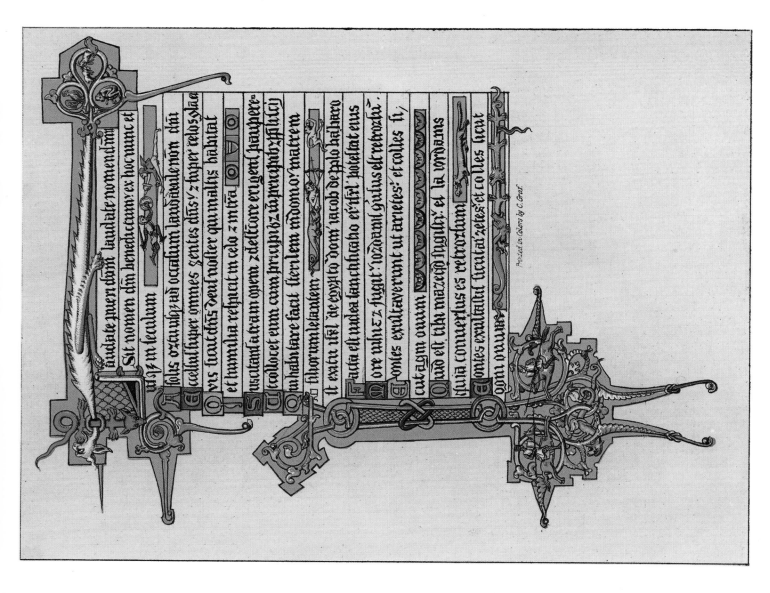

THE "HOURS" OF THE DUKE OF ANJOU

IN THE BIBLIOTHEQUE DU ROI, PARIS.

THIS manuscript belongs to the end of the fourteenth century, probably about the year 1380; it is an example of one of the richest styles to which the class of design that has been called the ivy-leaf pattern belongs. This style, which first appeared as a well-defined style about the beginning of the fourteenth century, soon became very general. At first it was very simple, consisting generally of a gold bar dividing into two branches of ivy-leaves at each extremity; these branches gradually became more complicated in their ramifications, and eventually broke out in various parts of the bar, as in our example. These extra branches soon became decorated with birds and other small objects, and subsequently, as in the missal known as the "small hours" of Jean Duc de Berri, with quaintly-conceived monstrosities, composed partly of the human figure, and partly of some beast, or some other object still more incongruous. Another feature in the last epoch of the ivy-leaf style was extraordinarily intricate circular convolutions of the branches at the exterior angles of the pages, as in the magnificent volume known as the "great hours" of the same Duc de Berri, both in the Bibliotheque du Roi, Paris.

But to return to the description of the volume containing our present specimen; it is profusely decorated throughout with borderings in the style of the page given as a specimen; and of miniatures, which at this period were remarkable for their beauty, there is an absolute profusion, the whole of them very expressive, and even fine in design, of which the one on our specimen page may be cited as an example; the positions of several of the figures being highly characteristic, and that of the female figure behind the Virgin really grand, as expressive of frantic grief. To those acquainted with illuminated miniatures of the best class of this period, it is perhaps needless to observe that those in this exquisite volume are wrought with the most minute and extraordinary degree of accuracy of line, and high finish. The damask patterns of the backgrounds, another marked feature of this peculiar period, are also wrought with the most elaborate care, some in blue, and some in red, and all varying in their intricate and lace-like patterns. In our specimen page the arms of Berri— field azure, semé of fleur-de-lis, with an engrailed boder, gules, &c.—occupy the open space within the capital G. The arms of Anjou occur in other parts of the volume. . This exquisite volume formed part of the great La Valliere collection, in the catalogue of which it is minutely described. At the sale of that collection it passed into the Bibliotheque du Roi.

onuerte noz deus salutaris
noster, Et auerte iram tua
a nobis Deus in adinto
num meum intende Do
mine ad adiuuandum me festina Glo
ria patri et filio et spiritui sancto Sicut

THE SALISBURY BOOK,

A MAGNIFICENT LECTIONARIUM, IN THE BRITISH MUSEUM.

A GREAT portion of this fine manuscript has been lost, but from what remains it appears that every page was richly illuminated in the style of the annexed specimen. From the dimensions of the volume, an immense folio, the size of the writing, and the original character of the decorations, this book forms one of the finest and most interesting existing monuments of the art of illumination at the close of the fourteenth century. Some of the features of ornament, and their mode of introduction, are quite peculiar to this manuscript, and will be referred to more in detail in the accompanying text of this work.

This book was executed for John Lord Lovell, of Tichmersh,* for the purpose of presentation to the Cathedral Church of Salisbury, as appears by a large miniature at the commencement of the volume, representing the Lord Lovell in the act of receiving the book from the friar John Sifrewas ; the miniature bearing an inscription on a scrolled label to this effect : —" Pray for the soul of the Lord Lovell, who ordered this book for the Cathedral Church of Sarum, for the spiritual memory of himself and his wife." The Latin is abbreviated, as, " Orate pro ana dñi Lovell qui huc libru ordinavit ecclie Catthedrali Sar' p' spuali memoria sui et uxoris;" which should read, " Orate pro anima domini Lovell qui hunc librum ordinavit ecclesie Catthedrali Sarum pro spirituali memoria sui et uxoris."

The volume was most probably partially destroyed and removed from Salisbury at the suppression of the Monasteries, in the reign of Henry VIII. By an inscription and pedigree inserted at the end of the volume in the year 1600, it appears to have been subsequently discovered by Joseph Holland, of the Inner Temple, a descendant of Lord Lovell, with whose family, however, it did not remain, for we find an accurate description of it in the sale catalogue of the books of " Mr. Thomas Grainger, gent.," dated 1732, at which sale it was doubtless purchased by Edward Harley, second Earl of Oxford, of that name; and, with the whole of the Harleian collection, it came eventually to the British Museum.

The page contains the last few words of some foregoing sentence, and then a portion of the " Sermon on the Mount," beginning Matt., ch. v., ver. 1 :—" In those days (it reads), seeing the multitudes, Jesus ascended into a mountain ;" after this it continues as in the usual version, with the exception of inverting the order of the verses, beginning—" Blessed are the meek ;" and " Blessed are they that mourn." The Latin, without the abbreviations, should read :—

> " me in ipsis sit, et ego in eis   *in die evangelium*
> in illo tempore   *St. Matheum*
> videns turbas ihesus : as-
> cendit in montem et
> cum sedisset: accesserunt
> ad eum discipuli ejus. Et apereriens os suum do-
> -cebat eos dicens. Beati pauperes spiritu quoniam
> ipsorum est regnum celorum. Beati mites quoniam
> ipsi possidebunt terram. Beati qui lugent
> quoniam ipsi consolabuntur. Beati qui esuriunt et
> siciunt justiciam quoniam ipsi saturabuntur. Bea-
> -ti misericordes ; quoniam ipsi miseracordiam consequentur.
> Beati mundo corde, quoniam ipsi deum videbunt.
> Beati pacifici quoniam filii dei vocabuntur."

The niche containing the two figures, with its long slender support, is intended to form the letter I, beginning the words " In illo"—its form, however, is rendered less apparent by the addition of the square picture, containing " all the Saints," and the " Virgin" enthroned in the midst ; referred to in the labels held by the male and female figures in the niche ; which are evidently intended for the Lord and Lady Lovell. The scroll of the male figure has, " Pray for us, all ye saints of God"—(Orate pro nobis omnes sancti Dei). That of the female figure has, " May the Virgin bless us with our relations"—(Nos cum parentibus benedicat Virgo). The scroll on the top is, " As a lily among thorns, so is my love among the daughters"—(Sicut lilia inter spinas, sic amica mea inter filias)—Solomon's Song, ch. ii., ver. 2. The scroll held by the angel has, " In honour of the blessed Virgin and all the saints"—(In honore beate Marie et omnium sanctorum); in allusion to the prayers of the two principal figures. The whole design, as well as that of all the other decorations, was most probably arranged under the special direction of the Lord Lovell himself, as seems implied by the word *ordinavit* in the scroll accompanying the large portraits at the commencement of the volume ;—the friar Sifrewas, there depicted, being most probably the artist illuminator who thus carried out the suggestions of his patron.

∗ The will of this Lord Lovell is dated 1408, in the ninth of Henry IV.

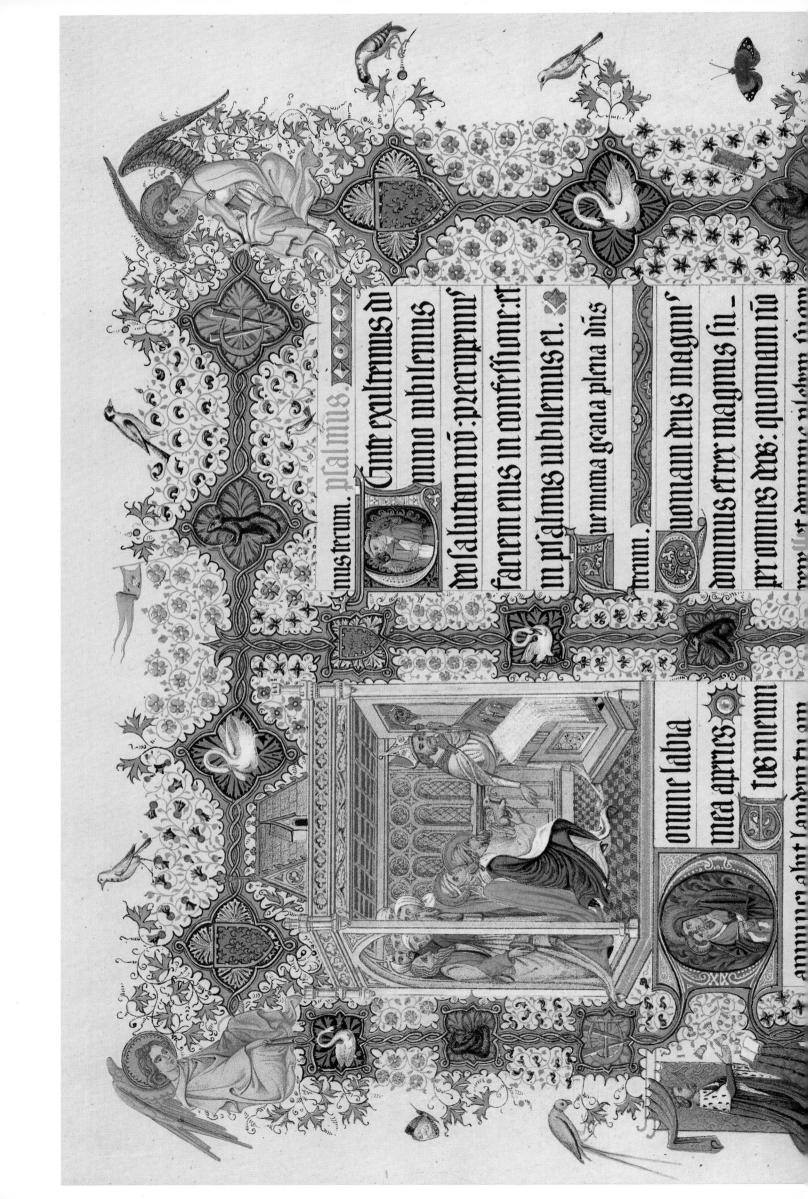

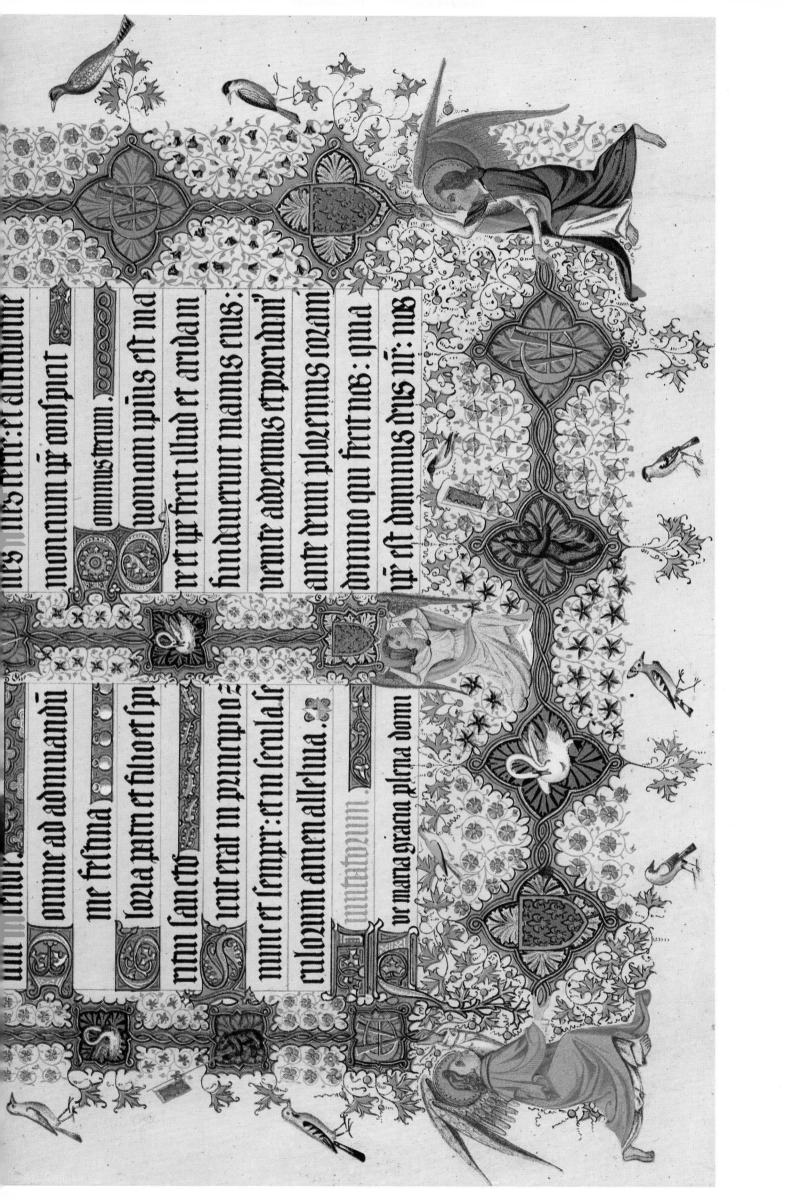

Be
ATVSVIRQVINON
ABIITINCONSILIOIMPIO
RVM.

LES MERVEILLES DU MONDE,

IN THE BIBLIOTHEQUE ROYALE, PARIS.

F all the treasures of the illuminator's art preserved in the Bibliothèque Royale, none is more worthy of careful examination than the volume in question ; a present from Jean ' Sans Peur,' Duke of Burgundy, to his uncle the Duke of Berri ; executed, doubtless, between 1404, the year of his accession to the title, and 1419, when he was assassinated at Montereau. It is mentioned by Silvestre as " one of the finest monuments of the period ;" and we may readily suppose, that a book intended as a present to the Duke of Berri, at once the most distinguished connoisseur and most munificent patron of art of the age, was confided to an illuminator of the highest talent, with directions to spare no labour in its embellishment. The book, which is entitled " Les Merveilles du Monde," contains the travels, &c. &c. of Marco Polo, Mandeville, Frere Oderic Mineur, and others ; and every page of it has been decorated by the artist with illuminated ornaments more or less rich. The ordinary pages are in the same style as most works of the period, of which the border attached to this description will convey a good general idea : but the pages forming the commencement of each book are quite peculiar in design, and unlike anything else of the period that I have seen. The one which I have selected to illustrate this work, though not the most rich and unusual in its character, presents perhaps on the whole a better idea of the illuminator's general intention than any other single page ; while the fact that it illustrates an event in early English adventure, gave it another claim to my choice. Many of the miniatures represent the wonders of distant countries, in a manner showing that the illuminator was imbued with the conviction, that " travellers see strange things :" and others, representing customs and events in different parts of the world, equally display the anxiety of the artist to impart the full spirit and meaning to the extraordinary *facts* of the different narrators. Some of these old pictures are in a more loose style than the one in our plate, but all those at the head of chapters or books are fully equal to it.

GREAT additional interest is given to the miniatures with which this rich volume is profusely illuminated, from the circumstance that the artist has abandoned the very general custom of the period, of filling up the background with a tesselated or mosaic pattern, composed of small squares, or other figures, of gold, blue, black, and other colours ; which, in addition to destroying the effect of the composition, deprived us of the invaluable records of architecture, furniture, agricultural implements, scenery, &c. &c., aiding to compose the background of a complete picture. The miniature representing Mandeville taking leave of the King previous to his departure, in the plate opposite, exhibits, notwithstanding its defective drawing, a much bolder and grander style than the more highly wrought and more intricate works of the middle and end of the same century : indeed, both border and picture contain even something of the fine simplicity and decision of the well-marked and complete style of the 12th century ; from some fine specimens of which, either in stained glass or illumination, our artist, not impossibly, drew his inspiration. The writing is quite upright, and, as usual, more regular and neat in character than that which generally prevailed towards the middle and end of this century : and for those who shun the trouble of deciphering the old character, I subjoin the text as follows, with a literal translation. Above the miniature is, " Icj commence le livre de Mesire Guillaume de Mandeville ;" " Here begins the book of Sir William de Mandeville." Below, is the title of the picture : " Comment Mesire de Mandeville s'en ala oultre mer ;" " How Sir de Mandeville went beyond sea." Then commences a sort of prologue, as follows :—" Comme il soit ainsi que la terre d oultre mer c'est assavoir la sainte terre de promission en tres toutes les terres c'est la plus excellente et la plus digne et dame souveraine de toutes autres terres, et benoite et saintifié et consacrée du precieux corps et du precieux sang notre seigneur Ihesus Crist. Ou ly pleut soy enombrer en la glorieuse vierge Marie et prendre char humaine et nourriçon, et la terre marcher et environner de joies, et la voult il maint miracle faire et preschier et enseigner la foy et la loy de nous Crestiens, comme a ses enfans, et de cette terre voult singuliere ;"—which may be rendered pretty literally as follows :—"As it is thus, that the land beyond the sea, that is, the holy land of promise, is among all other lands the most excellent, and sovereign lady of all other lands, blessed and sanctified, and consecrated by the precious body and by the precious blood of our Lord Jesus Christ. Where it pleased him to be born of the glorious Virgin Mary, and assume human flesh and become an infant, and walk the earth and cover it with joy ; and where it pleased him to perform endless miracles, and preach and teach the faith and the law of us Christians, as to his children, and of that land desired singular, &c. &c. :" which is sufficient to show, if all the rest of the chapter did not exemplify it, that the main object of Sir William's travels was a pilgrimage to the Holy Land ; and that we are indebted to his piety, as much as to his adventurous spirit, for one of the most interesting books of early travel, though less extensive than the better-known work of Marco Polo. The illuminator has not forgotten to place the badge of the crusader on his breast, nor the gold spurs of knighthood on his heels.

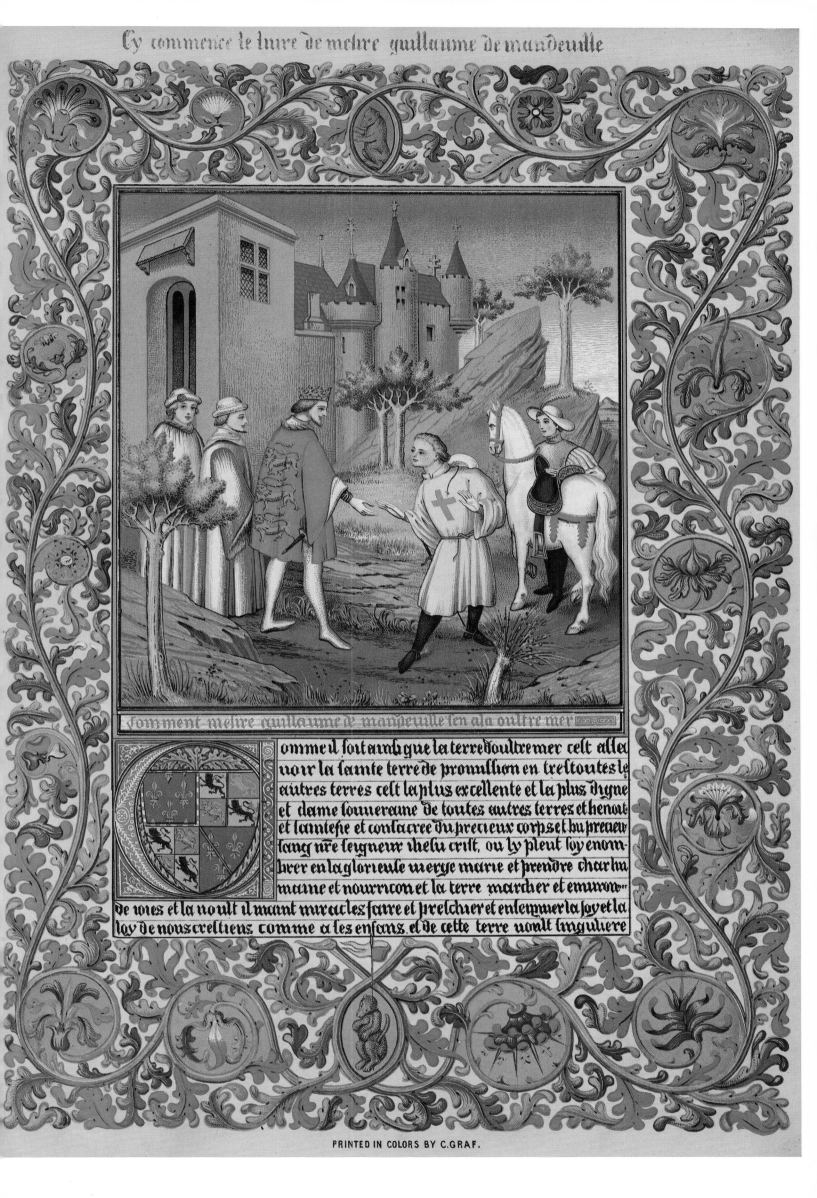

URIOUS varieties of ornamental detail occur in Italian manuscripts of the fourteenth century, but the well defined and elegant style of which our present specimen, from the Bible of Pope Clement VII., in the Bibliotheque Nationale, Paris, MS. Colbert, No. 18, is a truly magnificent example, is the one which was most general. The details of ornament are evidently founded on Byzantine models of an earlier period, as may be verified by reference to the outline No. 2, at the commencement of the volume, in which may be traced precisely the same forms and turns of the foliage. But in the Italian works the disposition of the ornament is entirely different, the florid manner of the western illuminators having entirely superseded the close formal arrangement of the Byzantine artists. The miniatures, however, and their mode of introduction, bear very strong traces of the debased Greek feeling, and are possibly copies of Byzantine originals.

The splendid Bible of Pope Clement VII. was executed between the years 1378 and 1394, during the papal schism, Clement VII. residing at Avignon; and from the archives of the cathedral church of that city this noble volume was brought to Paris, during the administration of the great Colbert, and still forms part of the magnificent collection formed by his efforts; it stands in the Bibliothèque Nationale as " MS. Colbert, No. 18." The first page, which forms our specimen, is a truly magnificent example of the peculiar and elegant style which distinguished most of the works of the Italian illuminators of the fourteenth century. It has, however, peculiar features of its own which are very unusual; for instance, the fine medallion subjects attached to the secondary borders, and more especially the central pillar of medallions, which separates the two columns of text in our example. These contain, for subjects, in succession, the six days' labour of the creation, and the institution of the seventh day of rest; the whole surmounted by one more richly ornamented, containing the head of Christ holding the New Testament. The deep border along the lower margin contains illustrations of the " expulsion" and other subjects from the book of Genesis; the whole surrounded by smaller medallions containing heads, and very gracefully treated foliage, which, as I have said before, though founded on the peculiar Byzantine treatment of leafage, is yet rendered entirely original by its novel adaptation to more florid and flowing general compositions.

The central pillar of medallions is connected by foliage, and a Mosaic background; it branches off very gracefully at the top, and is connected with the side ornament by well-designed leaves of an acanthus-like character. These side ornaments are very graceful, and give an accurate idea of the general style of ornament adopted in less rich manuscripts of this style.

The *marginal bar* attached to this description is from one of the less elaborate pages of this superb Bible, every one of which is thus decorated. It shows the marginal *bar* or *bracket* of the western illuminators, treated in the Italian manner of the period—the Byzantine foliage, so stiff and formal in its native school, being rendered playful and graceful in the highest degree, by the Italian treatment.

But there is another peculiarity which distinguishes this beautiful Italian style both from that of the Byzantine artists, which suggests its details, and from that of the western schools, which supplies its florid composition. This peculiarity is the distinct style of colouring, in which the place of the dazzling scarlets, and ultramarine blues (which are almost the only colours employed in *ornament* by the western illuminators of the fourteenth century), is supplied by a number of delicate tints which produce a subdued and chaste effect, forming a charming contrast to the vivid colouring of English and French manuscripts of the period.

These tints are, generally, a pearly gray, a light warm buff, a subdued but rich lilac, a pale pink, and a very delicate green; but the richer hues are not altogether abandoned, and in certain well-chosen positions still play an effective part. The employment of these subdued tints is more remarkable in this, than in any other Italian manuscripts of the period that I have seen. But the Bibliothèque Nationale possesses a smaller manuscript of exquisite beauty of nearly the same feeling—a book of " hours," also executed for Clement VII., and brought to Paris at the same time as the Bible.* There is in the Library of All Souls, Oxford, marked " VV 2 infra," a magnificent Italian manuscript executed in this style. But our great National Library in the British Museum does not possess a single specimen worthy of notice, as an example of this beautiful phase of the art; a deficiency which it is to be hoped will be remedied on the first available opportunity.

* See the List of Manuscripts at the end of the Introduction.

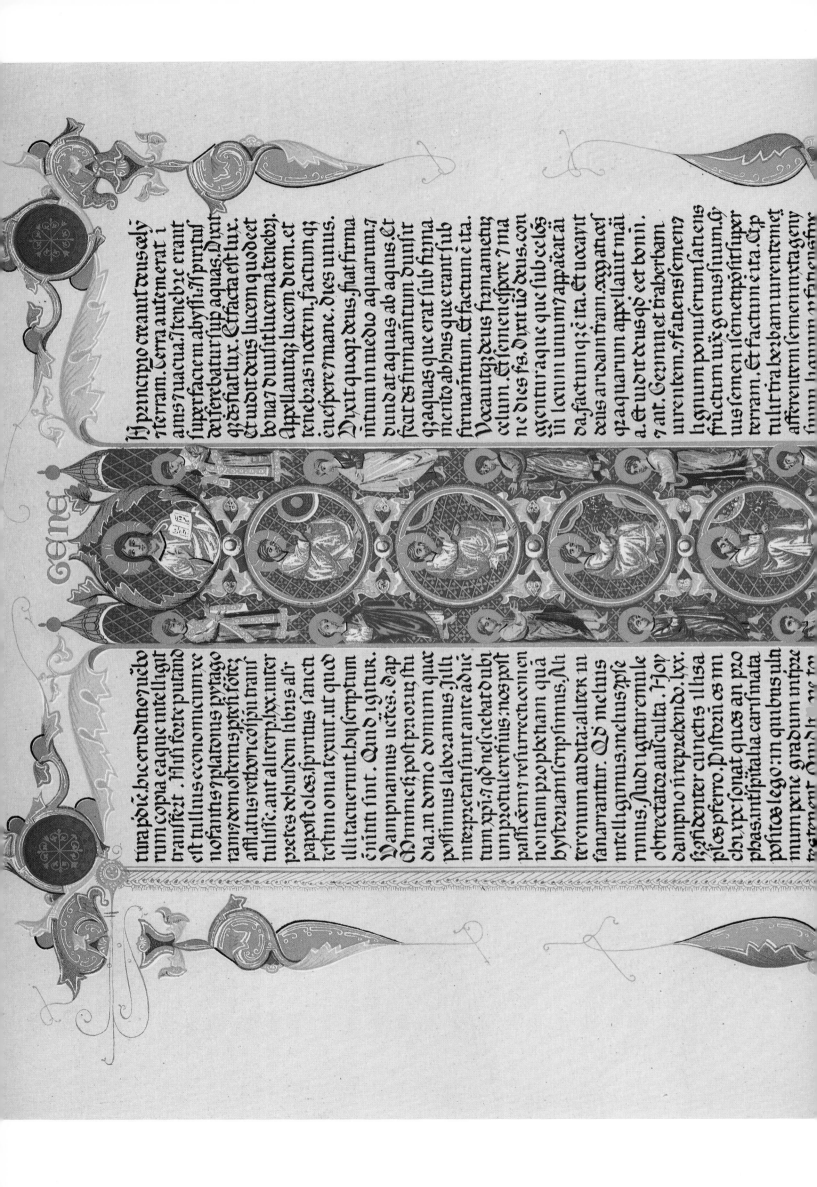

Genesi

In principio creauit deus celu 7 terram. Terra autem erat i= anis 7 uacua. 7 tenebre erant sup faciem abyssi. 7 sps dni ferebatur sup aquas. Dixit qs fiat lux. Et facta est lux. Et uidit deus lucem quod et bona 7 diuisit lucem a tenebris. Appellauitqs lucem diem. et tenebras noctem. factumqs e uespere 7 mane. dies unus. Dixit quoqs deus. fiat firma= mentum in medio aquarum. 7 diuidat aquas ab aquis. Et fecit deus firmamentum diuisitqs aquas que erat sub firma= mento ab his que erant sub firmamentum. Et factum e ita. Vocauitqs deus firmamentum celum. Et factum e uespere 7 ma= ne dies fs. Dixit uo deus. con= gregentur aque que sub celos sunt in locum unum 7 appareat a= rida. Et factum e ita. Et uocauit deus aridam terram. 7 gregacoes qz aquarum appellauit maria. Et uidit deus qd et bonu. 7 ait. Germinet terra herbam uirentem. 7 facientem semen 7 lignum pomiferum faciens fructum iuxta genus suum. cuius semen in semetipso sit sup terram. Et factum e ita. Et p= tulit terra herbam uirentem et afferentem semen iuxta genu suum ...

tura pdict. hic erudino quicquid um copia eaque intelligit transfert . Filii sortem putand et tullius economicum xc nofaiths 7 platonis pytago ram 7 demosthenis plenus fote, afflatus rethoricos pin tran tulisse. aut alter plox inter pretes rebustem libris al= papost oleos spiritus sanct rethmo ma texerut. ut quod illi tacuerut. by scriptum siuit sint. Quid igitur. Dampnamus uetes. Sap Dmmeqs post priora fñi dia. in domo domum quae possimus labozamus Illi interpretati sunt ante aduē tum xpi. 7 qd nesciebant ubi um protulerefius. nos post passiõem 7 resurrectoñem non tam propetam quā bystoriam scripsimus. Ali terenum an dita aliter in fanantur. Qd melius intelligimus melius ipse rnus. Audi igitur emle obtrectatoz ausculta. Hoy dampno in repzehendo. lxx. fzfidenter cunctis illi sa plios ferro. Distozios m cb. xps personat quos an po pbas. intipitalia cari finata pofitos lego. in quibus uh num pene gradum inter pa ...

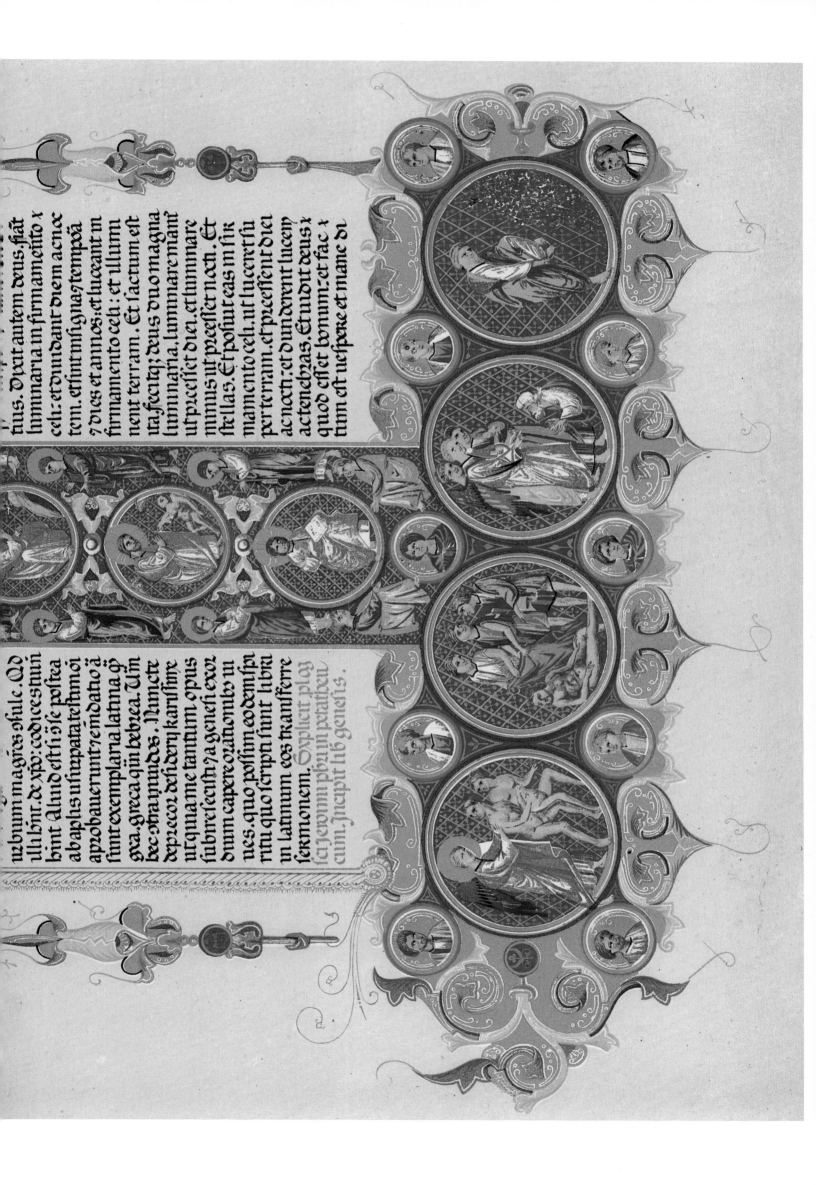

LYDGATE'S LIFE OF ST. EDMUND,

IN THE HARLEIAN COLLECTION, BRITISH MUSEUM.

THE remarkable manuscript from which our present specimen is taken was executed, by order of the Abbot Curteis, of Bury St. Edmund's, in the year 1433, as a present to King Henry VI., who, being then about twelve years of age, passed his Christmas at that abbey. The volume consists of the poet Lydgate's translation into English of the Latin Legends of St. Edmund, king of the East Angles, and St. Fremund. The former legend is attributed to Abbo Floriacensis, who came to England to communicate with St. Dunstan, a few years before the death of that saint, who related to him the facts of the legend, as he had heard them himself, from an old man, who had been sword-bearer to the canonised king.

One of the first illuminations represents a miraculous banner, said to have belonged to St. Edmund, and which, if possessed by King Henry VI., it is stated, would have enabled him to overcome all his enemies. The banner represents the "Temptation in Paradise," in silver upon a blue ground. There is also a picture of another miraculous banner, symbolising the most remarkable virtues of St. Edmund by three crowns.

The miniature pictures are exceedingly numerous, and executed in a peculiar style that I have never met with in any other book. The costumes are drawn with the greatest care, the dresses having very generally a rich damask pattern, of a dark neutral colour, upon a white ground, producing a sober but rich effect, of a character very unusual in illuminated miniatures of the period. It is considered decidedly a work of English art; as certain touches of white body colour, especially remarkable in these paintings, particularly about the eyes, are only found in illuminations known to be English.

These miniatures present a very high character of art (as applied to illumination), and though inferior in high finish and brilliant colouring to some cotemporary specimens, particularly the well-known missal of Henry VI., executed, as nearly as can be conjectured, at the same period, yet they possess a character of beauty peculiar to themselves, which is not less attractive.

One of the first miniatures represents the Abbot Curteis presenting the book to the youthful king, who is attended by two personages in rich dresses, most probably his uncles, the Dukes of Bedford and Gloucester.

The illuminated capitals, except in our specimen, are not large, and there are no other examples in the book of their being joined on to continuous borderings or brackets; but they are very elegant in their treatment and composition.

The specimen is perhaps the most highly decorative example in existence of this peculiar style, which grew out of the angular ivy-leaf pattern, about the end of the fourteenth and beginning of the fifteenth century. It encloses the commencement of the poem of St. Edmund, which may be read:—

> " In Saxoine whilom ther was a kyng
> Callid Alkmond, of excellent noblesse
> A manli prince, vertuous of levyng
> And ful habounde, of tresour and richesse
> Notable in armys, ful renomed of prowesse
> A semly persone, hardi and corageous
> Mercurie in wisdam, lik Mars victorious.
>
> " Eyed as Argus be vertuous providence
> And circumspect, as famous Scipion
> In kyngli honour, of most excellence
> Holde in his tyme, thoruh many a region
> But nat withstandyng his famous hih renon
> He so demened his hih noblesse in deede
> Above al tresour, to love god and dreede.
>
> " In wordli honour, thouh he were fortunat
> Set in a chaier, of kyngli dignite
> He koude knowe, in his roial estat
> Above alle kings, god hath the sovereynte
> And advertisid, in his most mageste
> That sceptre or crowne, may litil availe or nouht
> To him that love not god, in herte and thouht."

74

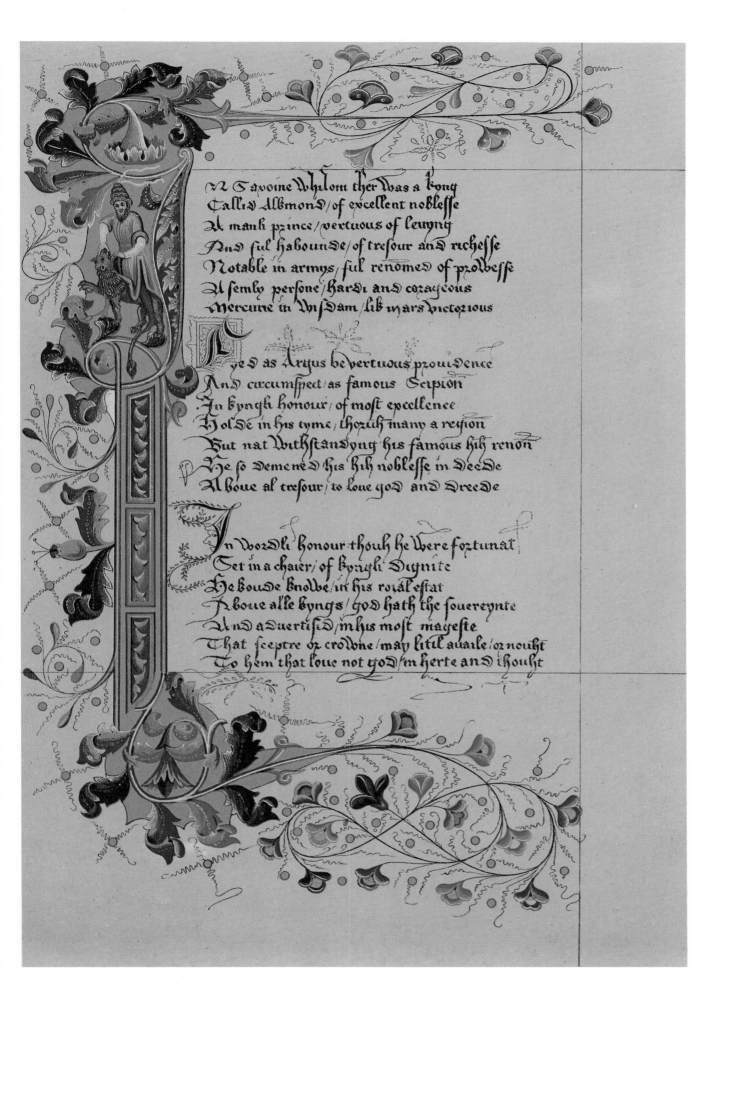

In Cayoine whilom ther was a kyng
Callid Albmond / of excellent noblesse
A manli prince / vertuous of leuyng
And ful habounde / of tresour and richesse
Notable in armys / ful renomed of prowesse
A semly persone / hardi and corageous
Mercure in wisdam / lik mars victorious

Lyke d as Artus be vertuous prouidence
And circumspect / as famous Scipion
In kyngli honour / of most excellence
Holde in his tyme / thorugh many a region
But nat withstandyng his famous hih renon
He so demened his hih noblesse in deede
Aboue al tresour / to loue god and dreede

In worldli honour thouh he were fortunat
Set in a chaier / of kyngli dignite
He koude knowe / in his roial estat
Aboue alle kyngs / god hath the souereynte
And aduertised / in his most mageste
That sceptre or crowne / may litil auaile / or nouht
To hem that loue not god / in herte and thouht

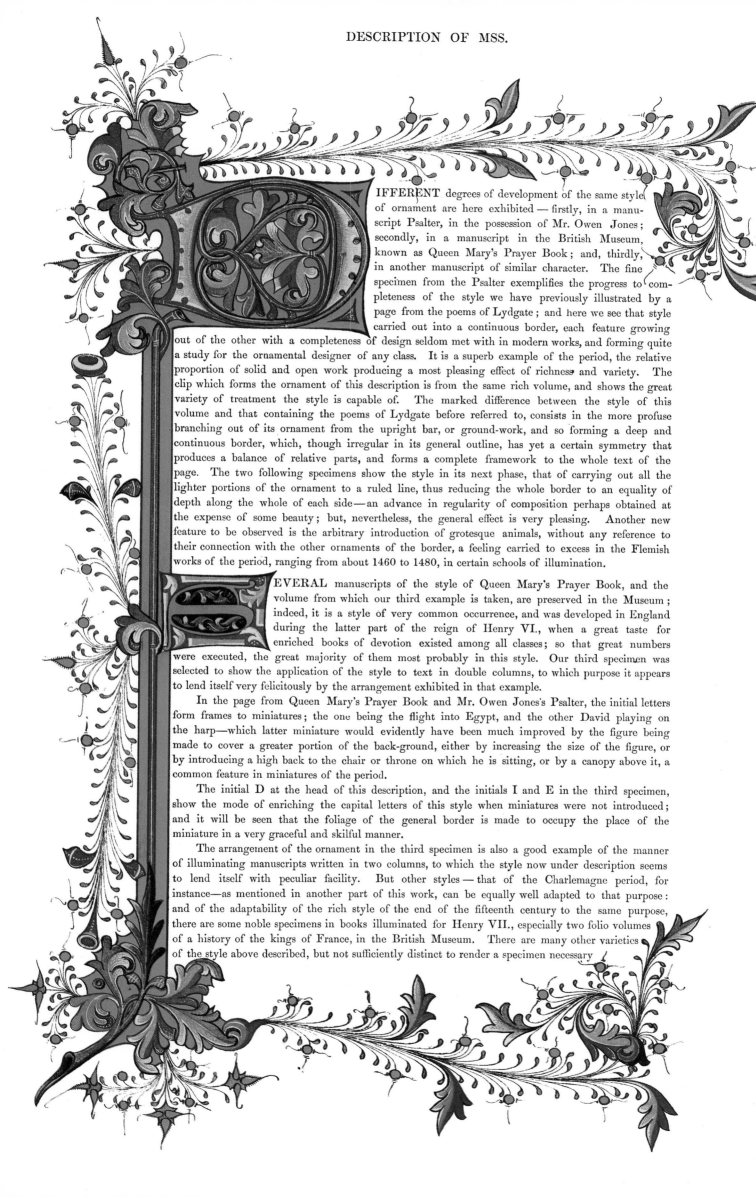

IFFERENT degrees of development of the same style of ornament are here exhibited — firstly, in a manuscript Psalter, in the possession of Mr. Owen Jones; secondly, in a manuscript in the British Museum, known as Queen Mary's Prayer Book; and, thirdly, in another manuscript of similar character. The fine specimen from the Psalter exemplifies the progress to completeness of the style we have previously illustrated by a page from the poems of Lydgate; and here we see that style carried out into a continuous border, each feature growing out of the other with a completeness of design seldom met with in modern works, and forming quite a study for the ornamental designer of any class. It is a superb example of the period, the relative proportion of solid and open work producing a most pleasing effect of richness and variety. The clip which forms the ornament of this description is from the same rich volume, and shows the great variety of treatment the style is capable of. The marked difference between the style of this volume and that containing the poems of Lydgate before referred to, consists in the more profuse branching out of its ornament from the upright bar, or ground-work, and so forming a deep and continuous border, which, though irregular in its general outline, has yet a certain symmetry that produces a balance of relative parts, and forms a complete framework to the whole text of the page. The two following specimens show the style in its next phase, that of carrying out all the lighter portions of the ornament to a ruled line, thus reducing the whole border to an equality of depth along the whole of each side — an advance in regularity of composition perhaps obtained at the expense of some beauty; but, nevertheless, the general effect is very pleasing. Another new feature to be observed is the arbitrary introduction of grotesque animals, without any reference to their connection with the other ornaments of the border, a feeling carried to excess in the Flemish works of the period, ranging from about 1460 to 1480, in certain schools of illumination.

EVERAL manuscripts of the style of Queen Mary's Prayer Book, and the volume from which our third example is taken, are preserved in the Museum; indeed, it is a style of very common occurrence, and was developed in England during the latter part of the reign of Henry VI., when a great taste for enriched books of devotion existed among all classes; so that great numbers were executed, the great majority of them most probably in this style. Our third specimen was selected to show the application of the style to text in double columns, to which purpose it appears to lend itself very felicitously by the arrangement exhibited in that example.

In the page from Queen Mary's Prayer Book and Mr. Owen Jones's Psalter, the initial letters form frames to miniatures; the one being the flight into Egypt, and the other David playing on the harp—which latter miniature would evidently have been much improved by the figure being made to cover a greater portion of the back-ground, either by increasing the size of the figure, or by introducing a high back to the chair or throne on which he is sitting, or by a canopy above it, a common feature in miniatures of the period.

The initial D at the head of this description, and the initials I and E in the third specimen, show the mode of enriching the capital letters of this style when miniatures were not introduced; and it will be seen that the foliage of the general border is made to occupy the place of the miniature in a very graceful and skilful manner.

The arrangement of the ornament in the third specimen is also a good example of the manner of illuminating manuscripts written in two columns, to which the style now under description seems to lend itself with peculiar facility. But other styles — that of the Charlemagne period, for instance—as mentioned in another part of this work, can be equally well adapted to that purpose: and of the adaptability of the rich style of the end of the fifteenth century to the same purpose, there are some noble specimens in books illuminated for Henry VII., especially two folio volumes of a history of the kings of France, in the British Museum. There are many other varieties of the style above described, but not sufficiently distinct to render a specimen necessary

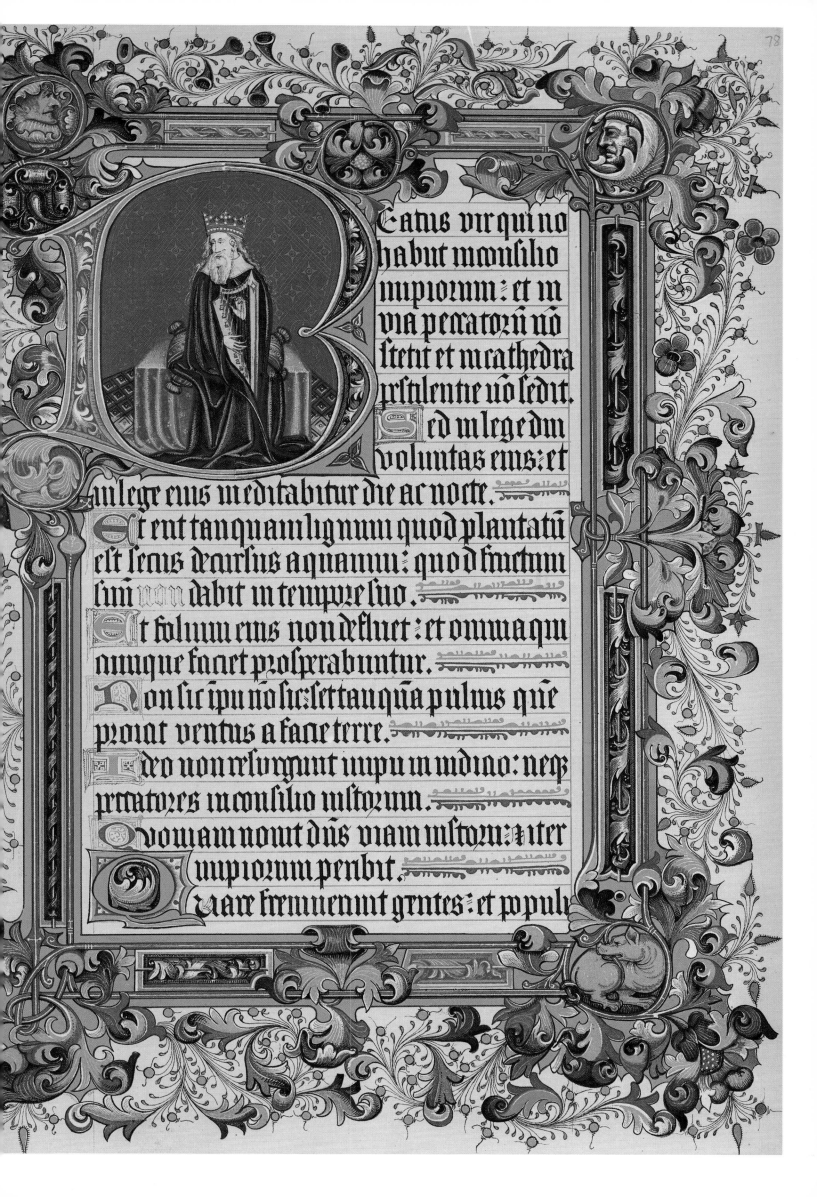

Beatus vir qui no
habuit in consilio
impiorum: et in
via peccatorum no
stetit et in cathedra
pstilentie no sedit.
Sed in lege dm
voluntas eius: et
in lege eius meditabitur die ac nocte.

Et erit tanquam lignum quod plantatu
est secus decursus aquarum: quod fructum
suum non dabit in tempore suo.

Et folium eius non defluet: et omnia qui
cumque faciet prosperabuntur.

Non sic ipii no sic: set tanquam pulus que
proicit ventus a facie terre.

Ideo non resurgunt impu in iudicio: neq
peccatores in consilio iustorum.

Quoniam novit dus viam iustoru: et iter
impiorum peribit.

Quare fremuerunt gentes: et populi

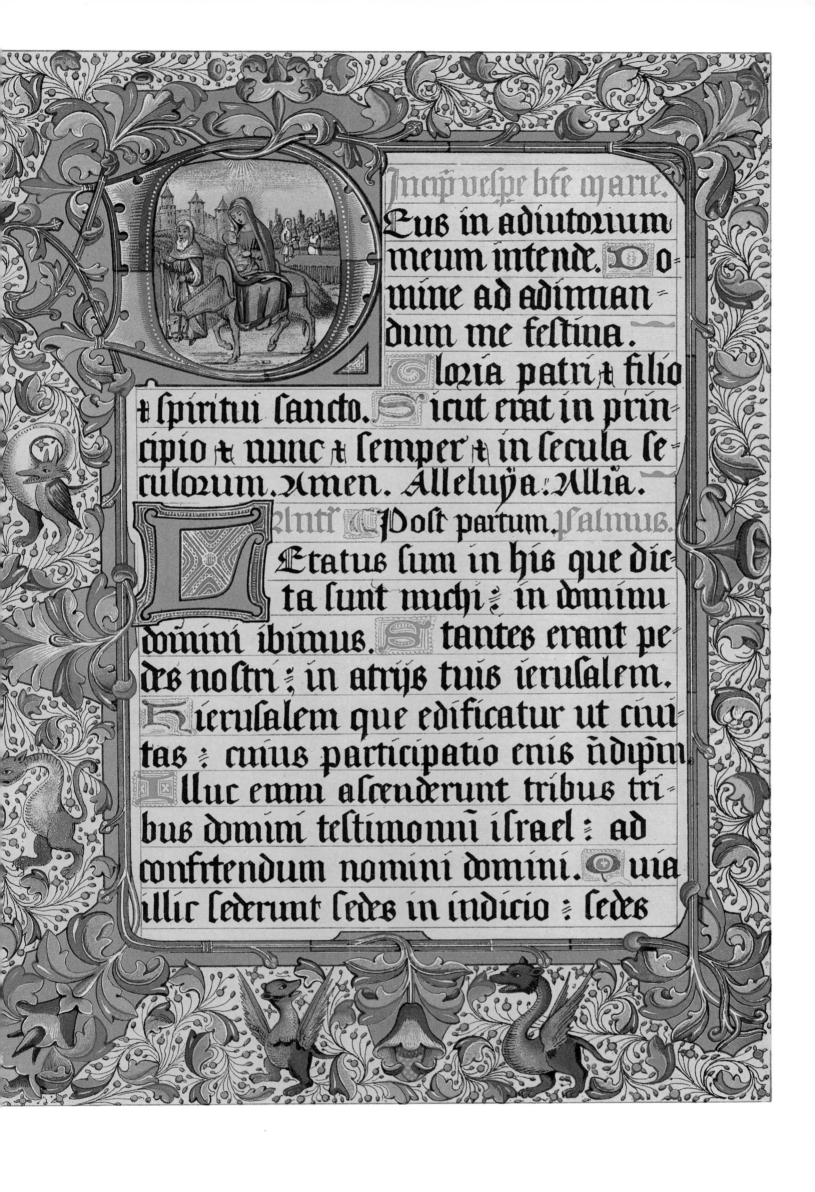

Incip vespe bte marie.

Eus in adiutorium meum intende. Domine ad adiuuandum me festina. Gloria patri & filio & spiritui sancto. Sicut erat in principio & nunc & semper & in secula seculorum. Amen. Alleluya. Allia.

lviiii Post partum. Psalmus.

Etatus sum in his que dicta sunt michi: in dominu domini ibimus. Stantes erant pedes nostri: in atrijs tuis ierusalem. Ierusalem que edificatur ut ciuitas: cuius participatio enis in idipm. Illuc enim ascenderunt tribus tribus domini testimonium israel: ad confitendum nomini domini. Quia illic sederunt sedes in indicio: sedes

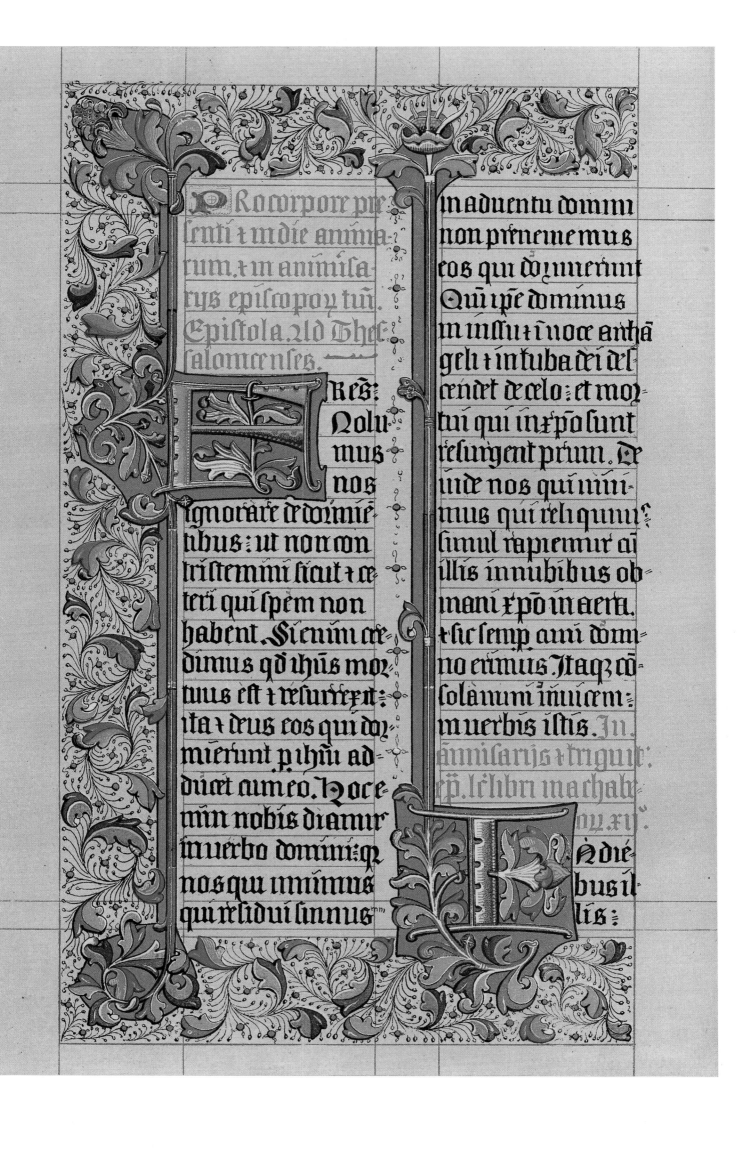

Ro corpore pre
senti ꝛ in die anima
rum. ꝛ in animisa
rys epiſcopoꝛ tuī.
Epiſtola. Ad Theſ
ſalomcenſes.

Res.
Nolu
mus
nos
ignorare de domie
tibus: ut non con
triſtemini ſicut ꝛ ce
teri qui ſpem non
habent. Si enim cre
dimus qd ihūs moꝛ
tuus eſt ꝛ reſurrexit:
ita ꝛ deus eos qui dor
mierunt. p ihūm ad
ducet cum eo. Hoc e
nīm nobis dicimus
in uerbo dominiz.
nos qui iuuimus
qui reſidui ſumus

in aduentu domini
non preuenemus
eos qui dormierunt
Qui ipſe dominus
in iuſſu ꝛ in uoce arhā
geli ꝛ in tuba dei del
cendet de celo: et moꝛ
tui qui in xpo ſunt
reſurgent prium. De
inde nos qui uiui
mus qui reliquim?
ſimul rapiemur cū
illis in nubibus ob
uiani xpo in aera.
ꝛ ſic ſemp cum dom
no erimus. Itaqz cō
ſolamini inuicem
in uerbis iſtis. In
annisarijs ꝛ triguir.
eꝑ. lc libri machabe
oꝛ xij.

A die
bus il
lis ꝛ

THE GREAT HOURS OF JEAN DUC DE BERRI.

IN THE BIBLIOTHEQUE NATIONALE, PARIS.

THIS magnificent volume is perhaps the very finest example of high Gothic art, of the richest period, applied to the art of illumination. It belongs to that particular school which was influenced by the symmetrical taste of the Italians; but only in the *symmetrical* principle, all the details belonging strictly to Northern art, more especially the French version of that beautiful and intricate style of decoration prevailing from the twelfth to the fifteenth century, which, whether in architecture, painting, jewellery, or book-illumination, has received the generic term of Gothic. The continuity and intelligence of character displayed in the composition of the borderings of this exquisite page is extremely ingenious, and the introduction of angels supporting the different portions of the exterior borders, from which the central one is made to descend, is of very appropriate and happy conception ; as is the manner in which the bands sustained by the angels are made, at equal intervals, to form Gothic medallions for the reception of arms, badges, and interwoven initials, connected with the house of Berri. The high finish of each of these heraldic miniatures is extraordinary, considering their great number; every page of the book being equally rich in similar ornaments. Among these medallions, those containing the swan will be remarked as exceedingly graceful. The intricate convolutions of the borderings to the calendar pages of this volume are still more wonderful, though not equal to the present example in other respects. The luxury of labour in the art of illumination was carried to its fullest extent about this period. Very soon afterwards such pages as the accompanying example only decorated the first leaf in a book, or those of the leading chapters, as is the case with the exquisite example of the style which succeeded this, the first page of the Comedies of Terence, exhibited in a subsequent plate. But there are many exceptions to this rule, and some of the most elaborately-wrought missals were executed as late as the beginning of the sixteenth century. The volume, of which the present example is one of the most exquisite pages, was executed for John, Duke of Berry, uncle of Charles VI. of France, most probably about the end of the fourteenth century, and from 1380 to 1400, as that prince died in the year 1416.

With many other richly-illuminated volumes executed for the same great patron of illuminations, this beautiful book of hours found its way, eventually, into the National Library of France, where it forms one of the chief ornaments of the manuscript department. A beautiful Bible, executed for the same prince, is now in the library of the British Museum, which though, comparatively speaking, but sparingly illuminated, is in some respects nearly equal to the present volume; but most likely, as the disposition to depart from the strictly symmetrical arrangement of the ornaments appears to indicate, of somewhat later date. The miniature at the head of the first column of our example is framed, according to the peculiar custom of this period and school, in a Gothic pavilion; which is always of some delicate tone of colour, varying from a light tint of emerald green, or straw colour, to all tones of pale pink, violet, or peach blossom. The capital letter beneath the miniature contains a neatly designed group of the Virgin and the infant Jesus, to which the royal duke, in the costume of a prince of France, is kneeling in prayer beneath a canopy.

The careful and well-marked style of the written character is also a very remarkable feature in this volume, and every sentence is decorated with an illuminated initial, almost every one being of different design, while many of the larger ones contain portraits of groups of most beautiful execution. A group of naked children in a larger initial on one of the subsequent pages is of truly remarkable merit as a work of art, for the period; rivalling, in natural simplicity of outline, the charming quaintness of the works of some of the early, but great Italian masters ; and appearing, as it does, upon a deep brown ground, the group has a cameo-like effect, very unusual in illuminations of this epoch.

The border to this description forms a portion of the decoration of another page of this rich volume. Though different in detail, it exhibits the same general principles of design, as that of the entire pages which form our example—the medallions being connected by a gold bar, instead of the suspending band above alluded to, give the same character of continuity and completeness. The stiffness which might otherwise result from the introduction of this bar is very cleverly obviated, by the convolutions of carefully designed labels, each different in figure, but all containing the motto " le temps Vendra" (for Viendra). The delicate filagree work, or minute foliage, which fills up the intervals between the medallions and scrolls, is of the most graceful character, and contains a greater portion of gold than the ornaments of the entire page, which are of a remarkable and somewhat unusual character in that respect. Taken as a whole, this volume may be considered one of the finest examples of intricate Gothic pictorial ornament, just previous to the period when it became irregular, or picturesque, in its character; the latter being a state of transition which accords with that in Gothic architecture, which is termed flamboyant Our specimen, from the Comedies of Terence, in the library of the Arsenal, is an exquisite specimen of the flamboyant style as applied to illumination.

DESCRIPTION OF MS.

THE COMEDIES OF TERENCE
IN THE LIBRARY OF THE ARSENAL OF PARIS.

VOLUME, containing the works of Terence, preserved in the library of the Arsenal in Paris, has furnished the present truly magnificent specimen. The book, as indicated by the royal banners, was evidently written and illuminated for a sovereign of France—possibly Charles VI.; but most probably, as the style of illumination would suggest, for his son Charles VII., during his early predilection for learning and the arts, fostered by the beautiful and accomplished Agnes Sorel, in the early part of the fifteenth century. The style of art exhibited in this work is that of the highest development of the phase of illumination that may be strictly termed Gothic; before the appearance of those new features which the revival of the taste for Roman and Grecian models had already begun to engraft upon the art of illumination in Italy, but which had not yet passed the Alps. The present illumination consisting of a picture enclosed with a highly decorative border, exhibits no trace of these innovations,—at all events in the border portion,—and may be considered, as I have said, a pure specimen of the highest degree of development of that style of art, which has been gradually unfolding its capacities since the beginning of the thirteenth century, and which may be generally termed the "Angular Gothic." In this exquisitely beautiful border we find nothing but strictly northern fancies; in which the picturesque association of flowers and fairies perform so prominent a part, and which are here so gracefully and artistically employed as decorative features: leaves expand to disclose a race of pigmy beings within their folds,—and flowers unfold their gorgeous petals to allow tiny standard-bearers to burst from their cells. Here, also, we see the northern heraldry of that chivalric age made equally subservient to the designer's will,—the emblazoned banners, not merely indicating for whom the book was decorated, but forming a beautiful portion of the decoration itself, with such infinite art are they worked into the composition. Then we have the tortuous labellings, with the Gothic letters, exhibiting the motto "De bien en mieux." These, and many other strictly northern devices, form this graceful border, the whole woven together and treated with that peculiar angularity and intricacy of outline which form the principal feature and perhaps the principal charm of the style.

The only part of the page which exhibits some leaning towards the classical is in the picture contained within the border just described, in the figures of which the illuminator endeavours to display something approaching to correct Roman costume, instead of the hitherto prevalent custom of dressing all personages in the common habits of the time. In this attempt, however, he has given us, to a great extent, his own notions,—modified, no doubt, by a reference to such authorities as were within his reach,—in the shape of bassi relievi and pieces of sculpture then still existing about buildings since swept away;—for it would seem that more works of Roman art have been destroyed during the sixteenth, seventeenth, and eighteenth centuries, than during the long ages of comparative barbarism that preceded them.

The circular form given by the artist of the Roman theatre accords with the form which he would see in the finely preserved amphitheatres of Arles and Nismes; and, as usual at the period, he has made his plan more clear by inscribing their names on the different portions of the building, &c., such as theatre (theatrum), players (joculatores), Roman people or spectators (populus Romanus), &c., &c. Below we have a singular bird's-eye view of a town (in which the laws of relative proportion are not much observed), with people on their way to the theatre, and others about entering it. By a section of one of the houses, Terence himself is shown, presenting a book, his last comedy perhaps, to a personage at the door,—probably intended to represent the manager of a theatre; or possibly the artist had a more poetical view of the subject, and intended to show Terence presenting his immortal works to the Roman people—a lasting glory to their language, even when it should cease to be spoken. The buildings are in the usual style found in manuscripts of the fourteenth and fifteenth centuries.

The book is written with exquisite care, and is full of illuminated letters, such as the A at the commencement of this description but there are no borderings of any importance after the first page, and the only other ornamental feature is the rather unusual one, for the period, of the title of the subject at the top of each page in ornamental letters, of which the letters E U N U at the head of this description are specimens, being part of the word Eunuchus, which occurs all through the comedy of the Eunuch, the other portion of the word being on the opposite page.

A FRAGMENT OF A MISSAL

IN THE POSSESSION OF MR. OWEN JONES.

THE two pages forming the opposite plate are fine specimens of one of the various styles of illumination that were developed in Flanders about the beginning of the 16th century. They were probably executed between 1510 and 1530, and are formed by a more symmetrical arrangement of the ornaments that formed the main features of Flemish illumination during the latter half of the 15th century. The picture, "The Bearing of the Cross," is in the style of Wierix, and is a good specimen of the art of the period. The medallion pictures of the border are new features, first introduced about the beginning of the 16th century; but the large initial, D, in the other page, still preserves the style of a preceding era. The borders are very fine examples of the ornamental feeling of the period to which they belong, recalling in some particulars, but much more floridly treated, the small prayer-book of the Duke of Anjou, executed as early as about 1380; but in this modern version of the style, the angular ivy leaves have been superseded by scrollings founded on those of the acanthus, as treated in Roman art.

The fragment from which our two specimens are taken, contains several leaves of a very fine manuscript, purchased by Mr. Owen Jones in Granada, which was doubtless executed for some wealthy Spaniard, during the Spanish occupation of Flanders.

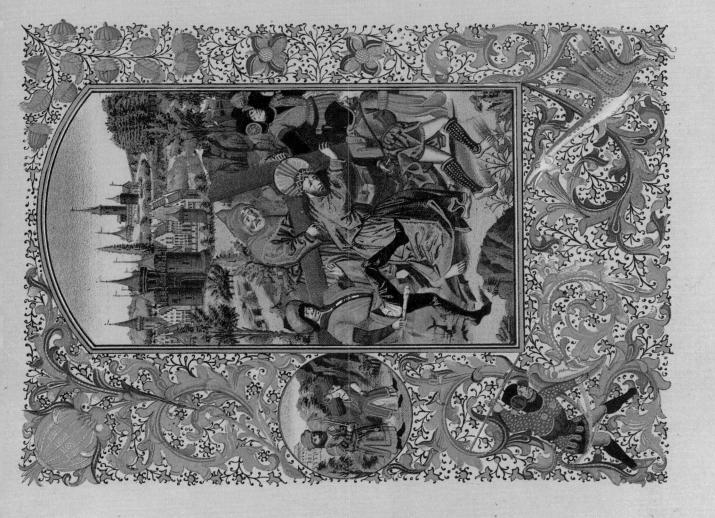

RECOLLATION OF THE CHRONICLES OF ENGLAND.

WRITTEN FOR EDWARD IV.

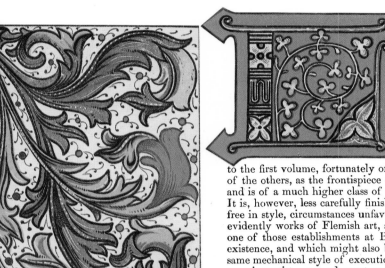

LOSS or other causes have reduced the original series of seven noble volumes, mentioned by the author, to three or four, now carefully preserved in the British Museum. The work was probably written in the early part of the reign of King Edward IV., and with the especial view of defending and flattering the King and the House of York, as will be seen in a portion of the author's prologue on our illustrative page where he naïvely states that he has undertaken this recollation of the Chronicles of England, " a la totale loenge du noble roy Edouard," &c. Each of the remaining volumes contains several magnificently illuminated pages, the commencement of almost every chapter being ornamented with borderings, and a picture equally elaborate with our specimen ; many of the borders are even richer, but the pictures are in a different and somewhat inferior style of art. The page we have selected to illustrate the style and character of this work forms the frontispiece to the first volume, fortunately one of the few preserved, as it is, on several accounts, more interesting than any of the others, as the frontispiece contains portraits of the author, and the person for whom the book was executed, and is of a much higher class of art, possibly, as Dr. Waagen has suggested, of the school of Jean van Eyck. It is, however, less carefully finished than many of the best illuminations of the period, though somewhat more free in style, circumstances unfavourable to Dr. Waagen's theory; nevertheless, the whole of the illuminations are evidently works of Flemish art, all of them, with the exception of the frontispiece, executed most probably, in one of those establishments at Bruges, which the great demand for illuminated books at this period, called into existence, and which might also be termed illumination manufactories. This page, however, does not exhibit the same mechanical style of execution as the rest ; but, on the contrary, appears to be the work of a different and superior artist, engaged, most probably, for the express purpose of painting the portraits from the life ; the fact which confers the greatest degree of interest on the work. From the individuality of character given to each figure, there is, indeed, every reason to believe that the portraits are authentic delineations ; a supposition placed almost beyond doubt, when we recollect that it was the almost universal custom of the period, when splendid books were commanded by persons of rank, to paint a sort of presentation page at the commencement of the work, exhibiting the portrait of the patron, with the author in a kneeling posture, offering his book ; the armorial bearings of the family being ingeniously wrought into the design of the ornamental bordering ; so that to doubt the authenticity of the portraits in this frontispiece would be to suppose the work an extraordinary exception to the prevailing custom, an exceedingly unlikely circumstance in the present instance. The figure on the throne is, of course, the king, whose commanding mien and dark flowing hair well accord with the received accounts of his person ; the face appears older and more lined than is consistent with his age, but when we consider his youth of great exertion and excitement, and the excessive dissipations of his early manhood, in conjunction with the truth-telling and somewhat harsh pencil of cotemporary art, we may imagine that we see a faithful, though hard and unflattering, likeness of the reputed handsome Edward.

FIGURE on his left, wearing the garter, is undoubtedly the unfortunate Clarence, whose vague expression appears curiously in accordance with his vacillating character. Gloucester stands boldly forward on his right near the front of the picture, also wearing the garter, but in no other respect resembling the figure of Clarence. He does not wear the long flowing gown or cloak of his effeminate brother, but is compactly dressed in a short close vest, and stands in the act of speaking to an attendant, with a determined expression of deep and concentrated purpose,—his right hand playing, as was his well known habit, with the hilt of his sword. The face, like that of his elder brother, appears too old, when it occurs to us that. on the day of Bosworth field, he had scarcely completed his thirty-third year ; but the number of events crowded into a short life in those stirring times, commenced on battle fields ere we consider childhood passed, the early development of violent passions, in conjunction with the strong linear manner of painting, are, perhaps, more than sufficient to account for this apparent discrepancy : the portrait, moreover, is younger in appearance than the one in the collection of Lord Exeter, and, as well as that of Edward, is in a much better style of art than the more celebrated ones of the Rous Roll ; in which they are introduced to illustrate the history of the great House of Neville, Earls of Warwick.

RESENTING his book to the king, the author occupies the centre of the picture, but his name is unknown ; the commencement of his prologue, which appears on our illuminated page, we give as follows, for the benefit of those who may find the old character difficult to read :—" Prologue de l'acteur sur la totalle recollation des sept volumes des anchiennes et nouvelles croniques d'Angleterre a la totale loenge du noble roy Edouard de . . . . . . IVᵉ de ce nom.

" Edouard par la grace de Dieu roi et de France d'Angleterre seigneur d'Irland pour ce que au commence-ment de toutes chose contendant a bonne fin. Selong la scentence des philosophes anchiens doit etre grace requise a cellui dont : "—which is sufficiently near to modern French not to require translation.

These volumes have continued to form a portion of the library of our successive sovereigns, since the time of their presentation to King Edward, to the time of their deposit with the royal books in the British Museum, of the now noble and still increasing library of which they formed the nucleus. The curious will not fail to observe an erasure in the commencement of the prologue on our specimen page, leaving a space after " Edouard de . . . . ," no doubt, originally filled by the word York. erased, we may conjecture, during the short return of the Lancastrian party, consequent upon the revolt of the Earl of Warwick.

The first part of these Chronicles contains a strange compound of traditional history mingled with the fable and romance of the early portion of the middle ages, not omitting the slaying of giants and marine monsters, with singular copiousness of detail. The portion from the accession of Edward III. to the death of Richard II., would appear to have been principally taken from the Chronicles of Froissart. We have not discovered any volumes relating to events nearer the time of Edward IV.; they doubtless contain, if still in existence, a strong Yorkist version of the war of the Roses. The border with which this description is ornamented, is from a richly illuminated page in the same volume as the frontispiece ; the L is one of the illuminated capitals with which every chapter is commenced ; and the two smaller capitals, A and P, are from the same volume, being such as commence every important sentence throughout the work. These specimens, with our large plate of the entire frontispiece page, will serve to convey a very complete idea of the style of these highly enriched volumes, a fine specimen of such illuminated books of the period, as were executed in the Northern portion of Europe, more especially Flanders, a style very different from Southern art of the same date.

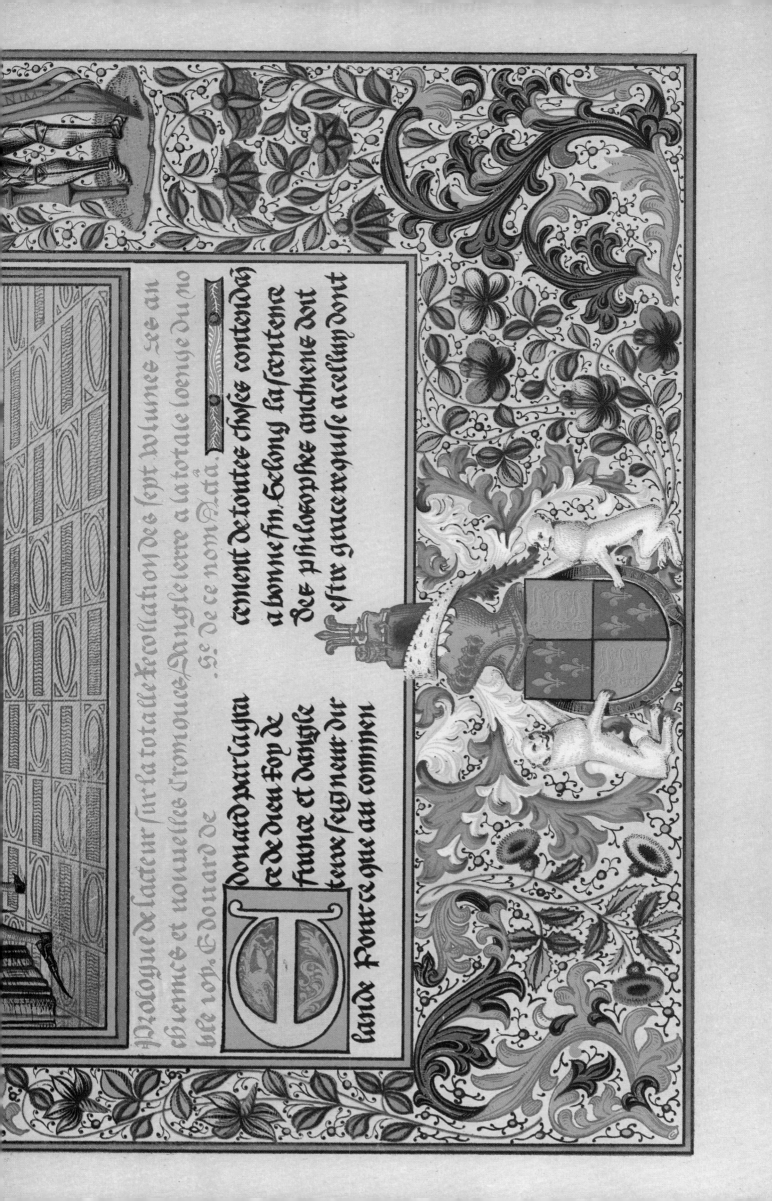

THE ORATIONS OF DEMOSTHENES.

WRITTEN FOR ONE OF THE FARNESI FAMILY.

NOWLEDGE of illuminated manuscripts, and the experience derived from frequent examinations of them, enable a student to assign the probable date to a work, at a single glance. This beautiful copy of the Orations of Demosthenes is evidently a work of Italian art, executed towards the close of the fifteenth century : an era when the discovery of many of the greatest works of ancient sculpture, that had remained buried for ages, was beginning to give a new direction to artistic taste. This new feeling, which was destined so soon to sweep away the elaborate and graceful fancies of that Gothic art which had produced those great European monuments, the Cathedrals—the pyramids of the middle ages, was followed out in Italy, the scene of the great discoveries of ancient art, long before it crossed the Alps. In that country, the cinq-cento taste, as it has been termed, had been in activity nearly half a century before the "*gout de la renaissance*" began to establish itself in France, and nearly a century before a similar reaction took place in England; where our chisellers were busily engaged upon the gouls, goblins, monsters, heraldic intricacies, elaborate fretwork, and other inventions of Northern art, about Henry VII.'s beautiful chapel at Westminster, at a time when, in Rome, the new and stupendous fabric of St. Peter's had already reared its classical cornice above the Corinthian capitals of its gigantic columns, and was fast advancing towards completion. This architectural comparison will not appear foreign to the subject, when we consider the close connection of apparently distinct branches of art, by some connecting link ; which may be illustrated by the singular chronological coincidence of architectural forms with those adopted in writing, exhibited in the simultaneous adoption of an angular feeling, both in writing and architecture, towards the end of the 12th century, when the pointed arch and the Gothic or German next, as it has been called, appeared together. As in architecture, so in the branch of art of which we are treating, the Italians preceded us in the adoption of the new style of the 15th century ; and the angular characteristics of Gothic design were still prevalent in the more Northern parts of Europe, while such works as our present specimen exhibit their total abandonment in Italy. Here we see mythological subjects copied from, or suggested by, ancient bassi-rilievi ; and the variously-coloured scrollings, evidently germinating from ideas gleaned among the frescoes of the Baths of Titus, or other similar Roman remains, which excavations accidentally laid bare about this period ; to which we are also indebted for the elegant arabesques of Raphael in the loggie of the Vatican, and many similar works in other Italian palaces of that date.

In the instance, however, of the bordering of the elegant page we are describing, the artist has not been a servile copyist; for the spirit of Gothic intricacy, not yet extinct, has evidently presided over his composition, producing a delightful combination of elaborate contrasts. In the relievo medallions. we sometimes find figures of gold upon a silver ground ; in others, the figures are of silver upon a gold ground, and some are entirely gold, relieved with a rich brown shadow colour. In the scrollings, too, we find a variety and florid richness not to be met with in the antique designs which suggested them, whilst the rich spangling of gold stars filling up the background is exclusively Gothic in its character. The whole of the composition, though not striking, from its small dimension, is full of graceful fancy and design ; indeed, the invention bestowed upon the great number of infant figures, all in different positions, and the variety of colouring in the flowers and foliage, lavished upon a single page of a little book, exhibits a love of art, both in its patronage and practice, which, in our manufacturing matter-of-fact times, appear almost incredible.

XQUISITE volumes, such as the present, could only be purchased by the rich, and this one was evidently executed for one of the Farnesi, a name intimately connected with the history of Italian art in the 15th century, the arms of that family being emblazoned in the lower part of the border. It was, at a later period, in the possession of the noble Neapolitan family, *Caraffa della Spina*, whose printed arms are pasted inside the cover; eventually, it found its way to this country, and was purchased by the Trustees of the British Museum. It contains but this one illuminated page, and some rich capitals at the commencement of the different orations, two of which, a K and E, have been selected, as specimens of its embellishments of this description. The book consists of some of the orations of Demosthenes, with the addition of the prologues of Libanius, a Greek author of the 3d century, who appears to have written these commentaries, or introductions, for the Roman proconsul Montios. The blue label, at the top of the page, contains the title, as follows :—

ΛΙΒΑΝΙΟΥ ΥΠΟΘΕΣΙΣ ΤΩΝ ΛΟΓΩΝ ΔΗΜΟΣΘΕΝΟΥΣ.

(Libanius's Introduction to the Discourses of Demosthenes.)

The prologue then commences. The portion on the page we have given may be thus nearly literally translated :—

" Since, O most excellent proconsul Montius, like the illustrious Homer, skilled in the powers of eloquence, you hold the first place in Roman discourse, and have, beyond dispute, obtained the palm in their learning, may you not neglect Greek literature, for in this also you may excel, by reason of the greatness of your genius; and, as you are learned in other authors, so also (may you be) in the works of Demosthenes, the most excellent of Greek orators : and since you require me to write the introductions to this man's orations, I will willingly obey your commands, not ignorant that there is more of honour than labour in the task."

The text, in modern Greek characters, is here given, as those of the manuscript are frequently rather obscure :—

" Ἐπειδὴ κράτιστε ἀνθυπάτων Μόντιε, κατὰ τὸν Ὁμηρικὸν ἀστροπαῖον, περιδέξιος τὰ εἰς γόγους ὤν, πρωτεύεις μὲν ἐν τῇ Ῥωμαίων φωνῇ, καὶ τῆς παρ' ἐκείνοις παιδείας ὁμολογουμένως τὸ πρεδβεῖον ἀνῄρησαι· ἀμελεῖς δὲ οὐδὲ τῆς Ἑλληνικῆς, ἅτε καὶ ἐν αὐτῇ διὰ τὸ τῆς φύσεως. μέγεθος ὑπερέχειν δυνάμενος. Ἀλλὰ περί τε τοῖς ἄλλοις διατρίβεις, καὶ περὶ τὸν τελεώτατον τῶν Ἑλληνικῶν ῥμτόρων τὸν Δημοσθένην· καὶ δὴ καὶ ἡμᾶς ἠδουλήθης τὰς ὑποθέσεις τῶν τούτου λόγων ἀναγράψασθαί σοι. Δεχόμεθα μὲν ἄσμενοι τὸ πρόσταγμα· ἴσμεν γὰρ ὅτι πλείω τὴν τιμὴν ἢ πόνον ἔχει."

We have not entered into greater detail upon the contents of the volume, or the style of execution of the writing, as the object of the present work is not so much with the literary or palæographical portions of the subject, as with the illuminations, in reference to their connection with the history of decorative art; and we have studiously kept these descriptions within a small compass, as the subjects will necessarily be again alluded to in the continuous sketch of the history of the art of illumination, which will be published with the last Number of this work.

A MANUSCRIPT JUVENAL,

IN THE BRITISH MUSEUM (HARL. 2,730).

ARIOUS distinct styles of illumination prevailed in Italy from the middle to the close of the fifteenth century, among which, that of the present specimen is perhaps most remarkable, as being totally different, in all its features and general treatment, from any other cotemporary European style. Its white interlacing branches, with their interstices, filled with grounds of various colours, powdered with small white dots, arranged in triangles, produce a peculiar effect, totally distinct from that of any other school of pictorial ornamentation. The feeling, as I have stated in another place, is perhaps founded upon an early style which prevailed in the twelfth century, but which was at that period confined entirely to initial letters, the practice of which may have continued in some parts of Europe through the thirteenth, fourteenth, and fifteenth centuries ; but I am unacquainted with any well-defined examples. Certain, however, it is, and proved by innumerable examples, that a similar feeling, applied to *borders*, was used in Italy early in the fifteenth century, where it was also applied to initial letters, some of which are very beautiful, and form occasionally, like those of the twelfth century, the only features of decoration to a manuscript. But I now more particularly allude to the enriched *borders*, which were at first composed entirely of white branch-work—in the earlier specimens *symmetrically* arranged, while in some of the later, as in our specimen, an irregular or *picturesque* arrangement was the one adopted ; and in these later specimens, compartments were frequently, though not always, preserved for small miniatures, &c., some of which are wrought with exquisite finish. Other enrichments were also introduced, even mingling with the white branch-work in late examples, such as birds in their natural colours, cupids, &c. The beautiful first page of a beautiful copy of Juvenal, which forms our specimen, exhibits many of these features, and is one of the finest examples of the later modifications of the style, that I am acquainted with. Yet much finer may exist, for the fine copies of the classics illuminated in this, and its closely allied styles, during the course of the fifteenth century, are numberless. Sometimes the branch-work is shaded with pale gray, and sometimes with pale yellow—of the former, our specimen page is an example ; and of the latter, the elegant V at the head of this description, taken from another manuscript of the period.

The latest phase of the interwoven branch style is that in which the branches themselves are highly coloured, the ground being of uniform tone, either gold, black, or some rich colour, of which the plate following this, from a magnificent manuscript, Aulus Gellius, is a superb example. Other examples exist, in which the coloured branches are transformed to cables, as in the truly wonderful manuscript in the Bodleian Library (Canonici 85), two outlines from which, at the commencement of the present volume, Nos. 7 and 8 convey an accurate idea of that modification of the style.

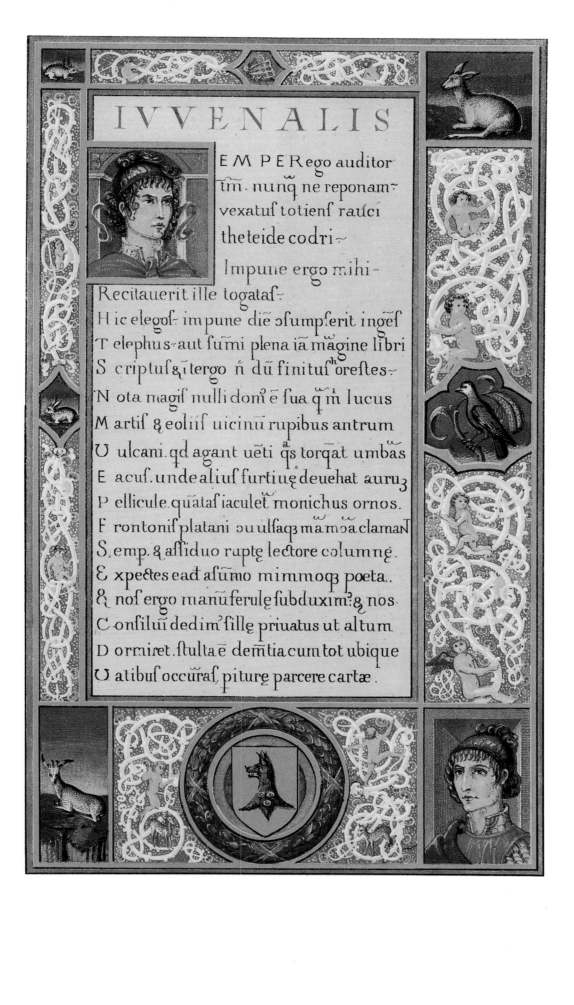

IVVENALIS

EMPER ego auditor
tm. nunq ne reponam·
vexatuſ totienſ rauci
the teide codri·
Impune ergo mihi·
Recitauerit ille togataſ·
Hic elegoſ· impune diē oſumpſerit ingeſ
Telephus· aut ſumi plena iā māgine libri
Scriptuſ & i tergo ń dū finituſ oreſtes·
Nota magiſ nulli domī ē ſua q̄ m̄ lucus
Martiſ & eoliiſ uicinū rupibus antrum
Vulcani. qd agant uēti q̄s torq̄at umbas
Eacuſ. unde aliuſ furtiuę deuehat auruȝ
Pellicule. quātaſ iaculet monichus ornos.
Frontoniſ platani ɔ u ulſaqȝ mā m̄ɔa claman
Semp· & aſſiduo ruptę lectore columnę.
Expectes ead aſūmo mimmoqȝ poeta.
& noſ ergo manū ferulę ſubduxim̄· & nos·
Conſiluī dedim̄· ſillę priuatus ut altum
Dormiret. ſtulta ē demtia cum tot ubique
Vatibuſ occūraſ, piturę parcere cartæ·

THE NOCTES ATTICÆ OF AULUS GELLIUS,

AN ITALIAN MANUSCRIPT OF THE FIFTEENTH CENTURY,

PRESERVED IN THE BRITISH MUSEUM.

THIS exquisitely written volume opens with the magnificent first page, of which the present specimen is a *fac simile*, as far as merely mechanical art can produce one; and, in addition to this, contains a profusion of the most highly wrought capital letters, of various design and character. The design of the present page is a carrying out, in the richest manner, of a style which originated in Italy about the fourteenth century, by giving to the interlaced ornaments of earlier periods a greater degree of completeness, produced by making the interlacings consist of positive branches, slightly rusticated with bark or knots; these branches were, at first, always white, or slightly tinted with yellow, the interstices being filled alternately with blue, red, and green, and at a later period, with gold also.* But in the present instance, the illuminator has sought to give the greatest possible degree of richness by colouring the branches alternately with the richest blue and green, highly shaded, and finished with deeper tones of the same colours. This arrangement precluded the possibility of filling the interstices with rich colours, as in the former phase of the same style, and the artist has recovered the sobriety of his composition by the use of a black ground, which is prevented from being harsh by means of a slight dotting of gold, producing an effect gorgeously rich, which, had it been continued all round the page, only interrupted by the medallions, would have produced a most perfect and original whole. But other parts of the border contain an arabesque composition of the usual Italian style of the period, which, though exceedingly rich and pleasing, yet gives an effect of incompleteness that, to a critical eye, is not satisfactory, especially in the lower portion, which appears too light to support the upper.

It is interesting to observe how ingeniously the Italian decorative artists of the fifteenth century worked the remains of ancient Roman art into their designs. The arms of the personage for whom this volume was executed, are supported by two flying figures, which might have been closely copied from those on a Roman sarcophagus in the Townley collection of the British Museum, and which may in fact, while yet remaining in Italy, possibly have formed the model of the illuminator. But the supposition is perhaps merely fanciful, as such figures supporting a medallion, or escutcheon for arms, are very common in Italian manuscripts of the period, and many other ancient sarcophagi exhibit such figures as the one referred to, though not so exactly like those found in manuscripts. They are, however, introduced for a similar purpose to those in manuscripts—that of supporting a medallion for a portrait or inscription, and are occasionally found with the medallion blank, showing that Roman sculptors of a certain class kept such works "in stock," adding the portrait or inscription when a customer was found. We may conceive that the first illuminator who struck out the happy idea of copying a pair of such figures from the antique, and making them a subservient feature in his own especial art, has been followed by a whole herd of imitators, who have perhaps sought out other ancient examples; but there is such a close resemblance between them as almost to favour the supposition that one original model has served them all, and that the model may actually have been the one referred to above.

The volume appears to have been executed between the years 1474 and 1494, as the arms are those of Ludovico Maria Sforza (il Moro), Duke Bari, who held the title during that period, and afterwards succeeded his nephew as Duke of Milan.

Great part of the library of the Dukes of Milan is supposed to have passed into France, and this volume was in the possession of the Chancellors de Rochefort, in the seventeenth century; and now forms part of the Butler † Collection in the British Museum.

---

* An account of this style will be given in another part of this work, in reference to a specimen of the white interlaced style.

† The collection of Illuminated Manuscripts formed by the late Bishop of Lichfield, contains many fine specimens of art, and now forms an important portion of the great national library in the Museum.

AVLI GELII IN OCTIVM ATTICARVM LIBER PRIM VS INCIPIT FELICITER·

LVTARCH VS IN LIB ROQVEM SCRIBIT GRAECE QVANTV

INTER HOMINES IN

terſit animi corporiſq; ingenio atq; uirtutibus conſcripſit. x ſcite ſubtiliterq; ratiocinatum Pythagoram phyloſophum \ dicit in reperienda modulandaq; ſtatuſ longitudiniſq; eius preſtantia: nam cum fere conſtaret curriculum ſtadii quod eſt pyſis apud Iouem dympium herculem pedibus ſuis me ꞏtatum: idq; feciſſe longum pedes ſexcentoſ; cetera quoq; ſta dia interraſ grecie ab aliis poſtea inſtituta pedum quidem eſſe numero ſexcentum: ſed tamen eſſe aliquantulum breui ora ſacile intellexit: modum ſpatuꝙ; plante herculis ratio ne proportioniſ habita tanto ſuiſſe q̃ aliorum proceriuſ: q̃to olympicum ſtadium longiuſ eſſ& q̃ cetera; comprehenſa a utem menſura herculani pedis ſecundum naturalem membro rum omnium interſe competentiã modificatuſ eſt; atq; ita ꞏid collegit quod erat conſequenſ tanto ſuiſſe herculem.corpo re excelſiorem q̃ alioſ: quanto olympicum ſtadium ceteriſ

ILLUMINATED ROMAN HISTORY IN THE LIBRARY OF THE ARSENAL OF PARIS.

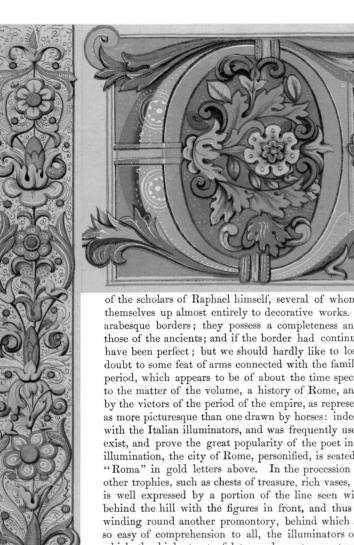

OMPARING the beautiful manuscript, from which this specimen is taken, with other Italian manuscripts of the end of the 15th and beginning of the 16th century, I am inclined, in the absence of a date, armorial bearings, or other positive indications as to the period of its execution, to assign it rather to the latter period. The Italian illuminators began about the middle of the preceding century to mingle portions of ancient Roman art with their composition, modifying them at times in their copy so as to harmonise well with their own decorations—at other times, blending the two styles so badly that a very disagreeable incongruity of effect was the consequence. It was not till after the practise of half a century that the true modern Italian arabesque resulted from the combination; and not till after Raphael had shown its capacities in his decorations of the loggia of the Vatican, that a positive and complete style was formed; and this occurred about the beginning of the 16th century, though tolerably complete specimens of a somewhat earlier date certainly occur—but rather in decorative sculpture than painting.

Our present specimen is almost the only one I have met with of the earliest development of the complete Italian arabesque being applied to book decoration; and I am inclined to attribute it to one of the scholars of Raphael himself, several of whom, it is well known, after the fame acquired by the Vatican decorations, gave themselves up almost entirely to decorative works. Nothing can be more perfect in its treatment than the composition of these arabesque borders; they possess a completeness and continuousness of idea that is seldom found in any decorative works, excepting those of the ancients; and if the border had continued along the bottom, in a manner suggested by the top, the composition would have been perfect; but we should hardly like to lose the quaint picture which occupies that portion of the lower border, relating no doubt to some feat of arms connected with the family for whom the book was made. The combatants are cased in the armour of the period, which appears to be of about the time specified above for the execution of the work. The picture within the border refers to the matter of the volume, a history of Rome, and represents a Roman triumph. A car drawn by elephants was sometimes used by the victors of the period of the empire, as represented on coins and other authorities; and such a car has been selected by the artist as more picturesque than one drawn by horses: indeed, a triumphal car drawn by elephants had for some time been a favourite subject with the Italian illuminators, and was frequently used in illuminated copies of the works of Petrarch, of which an immense number exist, and prove the great popularity of the poet in times nearly contemporary with his own. In the Roman triumph of our present illumination, the city of Rome, personified, is seated on the car, and the city itself, seen in the distance, is distinguished by the word "Roma" in gold letters above. In the procession are seen captive kings guarded by Roman soldiers, and captured standards and other trophies, such as chests of treasure, rich vases, and various spoils being carried towards the city. The length of the pageant is well expressed by a portion of the line seen winding round a promontory in the middle distance, which seems to unite itself behind the hill with the figures in front, and thus convey an idea of the great length of the line of figures; and it is seen again winding round another promontory, behind which a still greater extension of the line may be imagined. By such palpable devices, so easy of comprehension to all, the illuminators of the middle ages succeeded in imparting an interest to their miniature pictures which the highest art of later and greater masters has scarcely supplanted, for the realism of those old illuminations possesses an indefinable charm even for those who are cultivated to the appreciation of a nobler class of art.

The opposite page to the present is quite as profusely decorated, and the arabesque composition is, perhaps, more complete, being carried all round; but the ground being white renders it not altogether so rich in effect as our specimen; yet seen together, composed as they are for the express purpose of producing a fine contrasted effect, they form perhaps the richest opening to a volume that I have ever met with among illuminated manuscripts.

The borders of the rest of the volume never occupy more than one side of a page, and are by a different hand, in the common style of Italian illuminations of the period, but done in a bold free manner that is very attractive; some of the capital letters are very fine, and touched with great freedom, and others are peculiarly interesting as containing in their design the fac-simile of a Roman coin belonging to the reign or period treated of in the text, and these are finished with the aid of bronze or gold with so much sharpness and accuracy as to be almost deceptive.

There are also a number of large miniatures in the volume wrought with much more care and extreme finish than either that of our page, which may be said to form the frontispiece, or the first page, which is opposite to it. They appear, indeed, to be by a different hand, and if so, three, or perhaps four artists have been employed upon this elegant volume, which is certainly one of the most beautiful monuments of the art of illumination that I have met with, though perhaps not so absolutely elaborate as some of the works of the North of Europe of a somewhat earlier date. The border to this description is one of the general borderings of the volume above alluded to, and the large C one of the capitals first spoken of.

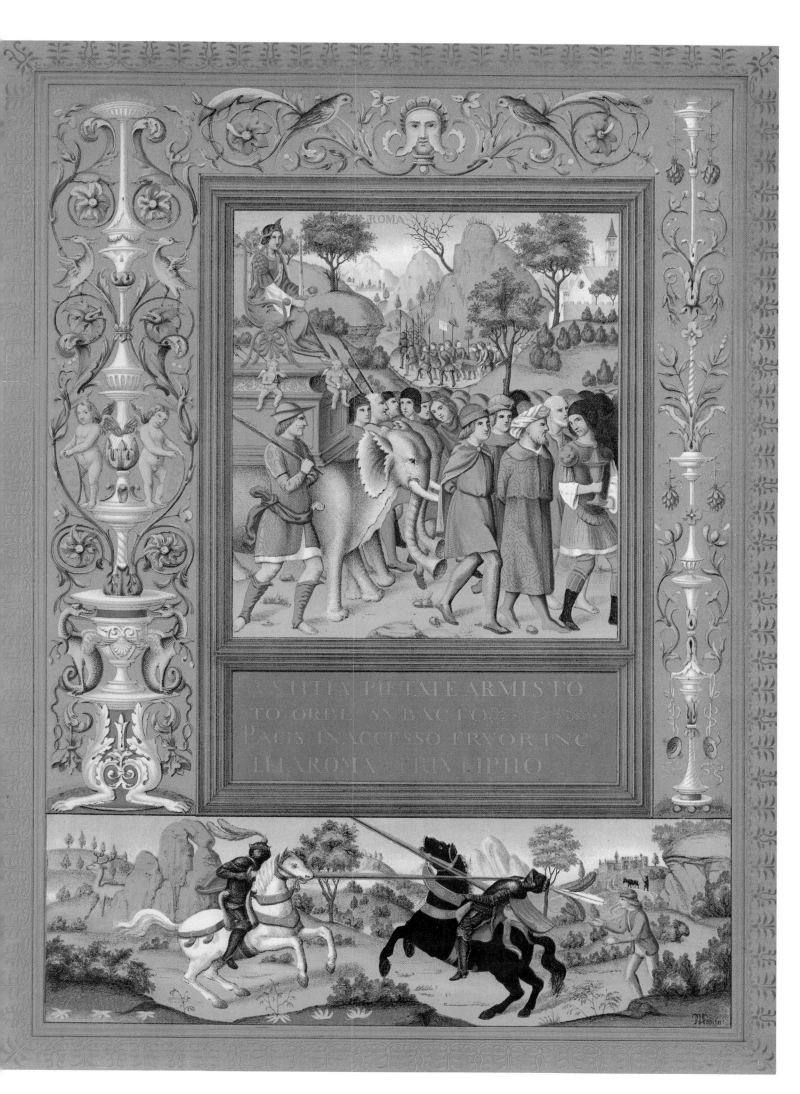

ROMA

IVSTITIA·PIETATE·ARMIS·TO
TO·ORBE·SVBACTO
PACIS·INACCESSO·PRVOR·INC
LIT·AROMA·TRIVMPHO

A GREEK COPY OF THE GOSPELS OF THE FIFTEENTH CENTURY,

IN THE BRITISH MUSEUM—HARL. MS., N⁰· 5790.

I HAVE given these examples of the latest phase of Byzantine art during the latter half of the fifteenth century, merely to show that that school of illumination never branched out into the various, rich, and remarkable styles, which distinguish the art among our western illuminators; but, on the contrary, preserved its original formal and heavy masses of ornament in their original positions and proportions, even to the end of its career. In the present specimens, we find the same square mass of ornament forming a capping or heading to the chapter precisely in the ancient manner, though the details are somewhat different; and the style of border or frame surrounding the miniature, though its burnished gold ground has disappeared, and a feeling of modern Italian arabesque pervades and slightly modifies its details, is yet the same as in the oldest models, in its proportions and arrangement. The miniature, however, of this particular example, it must be allowed, shows an entire departure from the conventional Byzantine treatment, approaching very near to the best class of Italian illuminations of the period; and this may be observed in many works to which the name of the writer or illuminator, Rhosus, is attached. That name occurs in the note at the end of the volume, of which the following is a free translation :—" The present four gospels have been written at the expense of our most revered lord, the Lord Francis, Cardinal of the Holy Catholic and Apostolic Church of the Holy Virgin Mary, by the hand of John Rhosus, priest and native of Crete. In the year from the birth of our Lord, One thousand four hundred and seventy-eight, in the month of April, the twenty-fifth day. In Rome."

Many Greek scribes and illuminators came to Rome as the fortunes of Constantinople declined, and the fact of this book having been written there, though by a Greek hand, may, to some extent, account for the greatly Italianised style of the miniatures.

Montfaucon, in his Pælographia Græca, speaks of the John Rhosus here mentioned, and says that he was a native of Crete, who wrote an innumerable quantity of books between the year 1440 and the end of the fifteenth century, which may be seen in various libraries of Europe. He further states, that Rhosus wrote a Plutarch for Cardinal Bessaroni in the year 1445, and says that Greek writing flourished especially in Crete, in the later centuries.

In the specimen, which in the manuscript faces the miniature of St. John, and contains the commencement of his Gospel, the form of the *capping*, or ornamental *heading*, by comparison with the outline specimen No. 2, at the commencement of this volume, copied from a work of the tenth century, will show, as above observed, that in five centuries the general style of Greek illumination had not varied; the small foliaged ornaments within the square are, however, entirely in the modern Italian arabesque feeling. The capital letter, it will be seen, maintains the same meagre character as in early examples (see outline No. 3), though slightly varied in detail, and enlarged (without being enriched) by a square framing. Nevertheless, the manuscript is an interesting and beautiful one, and in most exquisite condition, being as smooth and clean as on the first day it issued from the hands of the illuminator.

The Lord Francis alluded to in the note is Francis Gonzaga, son of Lewis III. of Mantua, born in 1444, died 1483. He was a munificent patron of learning and the arts.

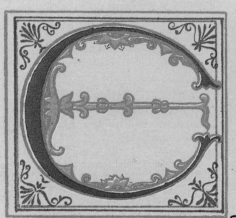

ϻ ἀρ χῆ ἦν ὁ λόϛος
καὶ ὁ λόϛος ἦν
ϖρὸς τὸν θεόν·
καὶ θϛ ἦν ὁ λόϛ
οὗτος ἦν ἐν ἀρχῆ
ϖρὸς τὸν θν·
ϖάντα δἰ αὐτοῦ
ἐϛένετο· καὶ χωρὶς αὐτοῦ ἐϛένετο
οὐδὲ ἕν, ὁ ϛέϛονεν· ἐν αὐτῷ
ζωὴ ἦν· καὶ ἡ ζωὴ ἦν, τὸ φῶς
τῶν ἀνθρώπων· καὶ τὸ φῶς ἐν τῇ σκοτία φαίνει· καὶ ἡ σκοτία αὐτὸ

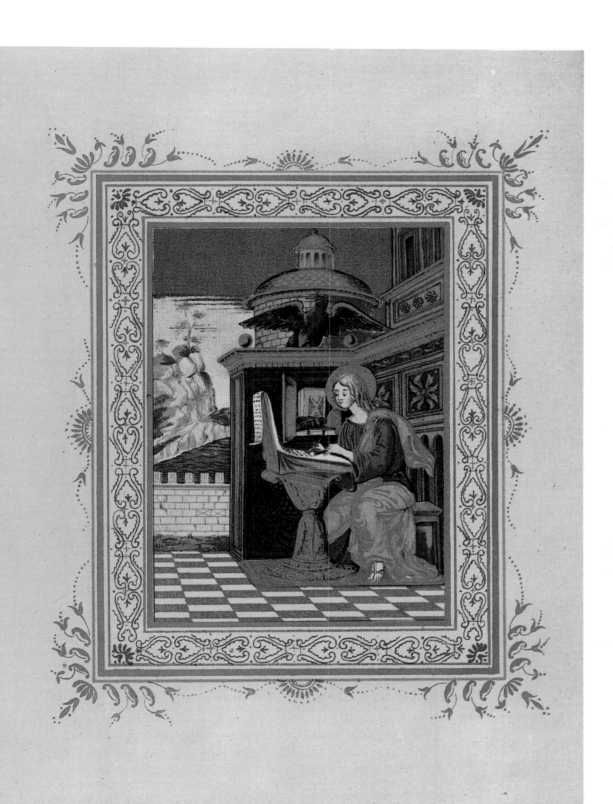

THE HOURS OF HENRY VII.

IN THE BRITISH MUSEUM.

N many accounts this is a most interesting MS., but principally as belonging to the last era of the true art of illumination, of which fine specimens are very rare. A portion of each border is composed of a natural flower, but so interwoven with, or rather growing out of, ornamental scrollings, similar to those used in heraldic blazonry, that the whole composition assumes the spirit of a *decoration*, its true and proper character, and is not a mere representation of a flower, which, in such a situation, would have been quite inapplicable. This fault, by the way, may be urged against the beautiful Missal of Anne of Brittany, of which examples will be given in this work, and the exquisite MS. of a similar character in the possession of Mr. Holford, — works nearly contemporaneous, but probably of a somewhat later period than these Hours of Henry VII. ; — in both of which, conventional ornaments are discarded, and the borders or framings composed simply of natural flowers or fruits.

The rich and florid style of the borders of this MS. corresponds exactly to the last cotemporary stage of Gothic architecture ; and I could name many oak carvings of the period, particularly some on the pews of Sefton Church, near Liverpool, which are designed in a very similar style, and might almost be supposed the production of the same mind, working for the carver instead of the illuminator. I can imagine a building of this period, in which the art of the illuminator, as exhibited in this beautiful MS., and the art of the carver and architect, as exhibited at Sefton, might form a most charming combination in polychromic art ; and such combinations doubtless did exist in this country ere the puritanic whitewash did its work of wide destruction.

I know of no other MS. of this style, though the Museum possesses one or two in some degree similar in design, but so rude in execution as not to be for a moment compared with it as a work of art. It appears to me to be most probably an English production, both from analogies above mentioned, and because, although the compositions exhibit much of the principle of the German art of the period, the details are not so crisp or varied ; whilst the rich scrollings with which it is ornamented clearly distinguish it from the style of cotemporary French illuminators.

The volume contains but a fragment of the original Missal ; and, although it came direct from the royal library at Windsor to the Museum, with the books presented by George IV., it has been strangely mutilated : so insufficient was the care taken of these rare treasures of the art of the illuminator till within the last quarter of a century. In a scrap collection, containing principally specimens of early printed letters, &c. &c., recently purchased by the Museum, several pages of this beautiful book were found, but with the illuminated borders cut out. The collector, it would appear, caring only for the pages as specimens of writing, the borders were probably cut out, as a pretty trifle for some female friend, to line a workbox, or make thread-papers with.

The two pages containing portions of the Psalms, &c. &c., which form the opposite plate, will convey an excellent general idea of the illuminations throughout the volume ; though the border of every page exhibits a different flower and different scrollings.

The border and capital O, ornamenting this description, are taken from the same volume.

e adoramus te venera
mur te benedicimus
o beata trinitas
Versus Sit nomen domini ben
dictum Et hic nunc et hoc quod seculum
ihesus semper oratio
terne deus qui dedis
ti famulis tuis in confessione
vere fidei eterne trinitatis gloriam
agnoscere et in potencia maies
tatis adorare unitatem quos ut
eiusdem fidei firmitatem ab omnibus
semper muniamur adversis
Per xpm
De corpore xpi antiphona
Sacrum convivium
In quo xpus sumitur
recolitur memoria passionis eius

conturbata sunt omnia ossa mea
t anima mea turbata est
valde sed tu domine usque quo
convertere domine et eripe
animam meam salvum me fac prop
ter misericordiam tuam
nomiam non est in morte
qui memor sit tui in inferno autem
quis confitebitur tibi
aborau in gemitu meo
lauabo per singulas noctes lectum
meum lacrimis meis stratum meum
rigabo
turbatus est a furore oculus
meus inueteraui inter omnes in
micos meos
Discedite a me omnes qui
operamini iniquitatem quoniam

THE "HOURS" OF ANNE OF BRITTANY

IN THE BIBLIOTHEQUE DU ROI, PARIS.

THE magnificent missal from which the two present specimens are taken, was executed for Anne of Brittany ; most probably on her marriage with Charles VIII., as her initials were interlaced with those of that king at the commencement of the volume. If such is the case, it was executed at the close of the fifteenth century, and forms a fine climax to that epoch, celebrated as the finest period of the art of illumination.

The volume has been overladen with extravagant praise by many describers ; but a fair and even severe estimate must assign it a position among the finest works of its class, if not in the very first rank.

The great simplicity of its ornaments place it quite apart from the common illuminations of the period; it is, as it were, the last word of the higher Gothic school of illumination, which had been long tending more and more towards the absolutely natural in the form and distribution of its main features, which, as mere ornaments, perhaps rendered them less appropriate for their respective positions than conventional forms. Be this as it may, in this style, the supreme effort of the art of illumination, nature, as far as lay within the capacity of the artist, has been strictly followed, and yet nothing of the highly decorative character lost ; though the pleasing angularity and intricacy and truly architectonic character of the strictly Gothic period has been abandoned. It may be remarked that the gold, upon which the objects appear, is no longer, as in the earlier stages of the art, a metallic atmosphere, as it were, in which the objects float without shadow, but is a palpable (and possible) gold ground, upon which each object casts a natural shadow, so artistically treated as to become in itself a decorative feature.

It is a style, that, having abandoned the quaintness and intricacy of the previous Gothic feeling, but without adopting any of the foreign features of Italian arabesque, might have led eventually to an original and beautiful school of decorative art, of which we shall never now be able to form any conception ; but which was crushed by the almost immediate introduction of the Italian style of the revival. Many epochs in the history of an art present a similarly tantalizing view.

But to return to the "hours" of Anne of Brittany, the volume commences with the calendar, which is written on tablets, placed in the centre of large miniatures (of the size of our specimen, the Adoration of the Magi), the figures of which are arranged so as not to be cut by the tablet.

They form an illuminated calendar, which I believe is unique, both as to size and beauty of composition. This is followed by the usual prayers, each either surrounded or bordered on one side by a gold band, on which is painted a natural flower or flowers, or in some cases fruits, as in our specimen, which is a page containing a portion of the service for the festival of the annunciation.

Some of these borders are of most exquisite finish, such as no mechanical process can imitate, and perfectly jewelled over with glittering insects, wrought up with the most sparkling brilliancy. In addition to these borderings, there is a large miniature occupying an entire page opposite to the prayer for each saint's day, and each principal "office," some of them of the most elaborate character, and approaching, in elegance of drawing and grace of outline, especially in the female figures, to the early manner of Raphael, though evidently the work of a native French artist.

In the bordered page, the *tint* outside the border represents the vellum of the original, and shows the exact size of the book. In the miniature subject, the entire margin has been filled up with black ; and in some others, an intense shade of blue, red, or green, commences immediately under the gold framing of the picture, and gradually dies off to the edge of the leaf—a manner not uncommon in Italian manuscripts of the period.

I should not omit to state that the first prayer is preceded by a large miniature of great interest, as containing accurate and elaborately wrought portraits of Anne of Brittany and several ladies of her court at prayers, in a style of art nearly equal to that of the great masters of the period.

It was long thought by the conservators of the Bibliotheque du Roi, that this manuscript was unique, but England possesses another in the same style, and evidently by the same hand, some of the fruit borderings being even finer than those of the Paris manuscript ; but it is without the calendar that forms so attractive a feature in the former volume : this exquisite volume is in the fine collection of R. S. Holford, Esq.

ET APTIS · THESAVRIS · SVIS · OBTVLĒRT · EI · MVERA · IVR THꝰ · ET · MIRRA ·

In illo tempore. missus est gabriel angelus a deo in ciuitatem galilee cui nomen nazareth ad virginem desponsatam viro cui nomen erat ioseph de domo dauid: et nomen virginis maria. Et ingressus angelus ad eam dixit. Aue gratia plena dominus tecum: benedicta tu in mulieribus. Que cum audisset turbata est in sermone eius: et cogitabat qualis esset ista salutatio. Et ait angelus ei Ne timeas maria inuenisti enim gratiam apud dominum. Ecce concipies in vtero et paries filium: et vocabis nomen eius ihesum Hic erit magnus et filius altissimi vo

A MISSAL

IN THE LIBRARY OF THE ARSENAL OF PARIS.

THE present specimens are from the calendar of a very rich missal in the library of the Arsenal, and exhibit one of the early examples of detached flowers strewed over a ground of gold, or some rich colour sprinkled with gold, as in the present instance—a style which commenced with the sixteenth century.

The artist had evidently seen the famous missal of Anne of Brittany, and conceived the idea of enclosing one of those pages, that are decorated with a simple band and a single flower, within a rich border of his own composition in the later style ; and the result is one of the richest though perhaps not the most perfect combinations exhibited in any work of the class. The exterior border contains medallions formed by foliated branch work, in which are painted miniatures of the different saints of the month, each accompanied by an appropriate symbol, by which he may be at once recognised.

With unusual luxury each month is made to occupy two pages, the medallion at the foot of the first containing an illustration of the rural occupation of the month, and the other the zodiacal sign—in this instance it is virgo, seated within a singularly managed radiation of gold work, that produces a curious and somewhat appropriate effect. The rest of the volume is in a different style to the calendar, no more natural flowers occurring, and the whole of the borders being filled with the richly foliated branch work which about this time and even a little earlier began to form a striking feature in a particular school of German and Flemish illumination. The miniatures are also numerous, but not of a high character.

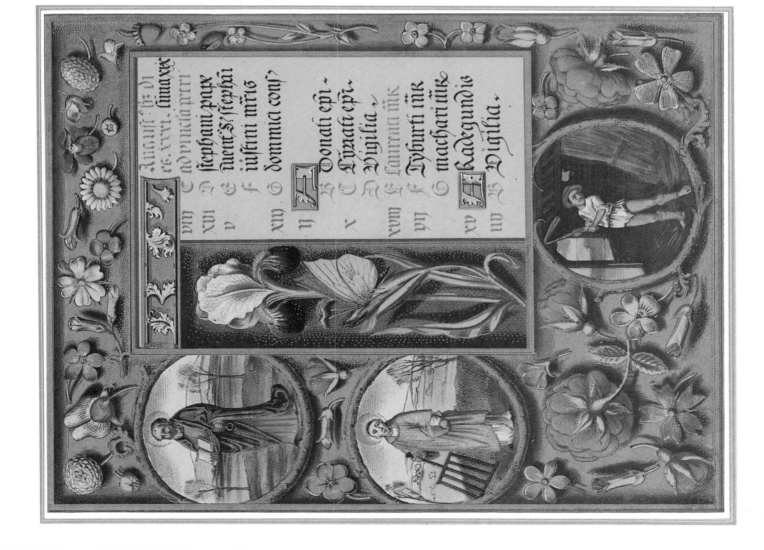

"LES HEURES D'ANNE DE FRANCE,"

PRESERVED IN THE BIBLIOTHEQUE DU ROI, PARIS.

THE "Hours" of Anne of France form a very rich and profusely illuminated volume, executed about the close of the fifteenth century, when the taste of the revival began to supersede the Gothic feeling in decoration, producing a great variety of mixed styles, of which this book is an example. Some of the borders are partly filled with the arabesques, formed of heart's-ease, daisy, and columbine flowers, intermingled with purple and red scrollings of conventional foliage, derived from the acanthus, which formed the marked style of the middle of the fifteenth century, and of which the page from the "Chronicles of England," in this work, may be cited as a good example, though differing somewhat from the most common examples of the style. Other portions of the same borders are occupied with designs similar to those in the present example, while some of the borders, of an architectural character, exhibit a portion of the design, with pointed arches and all the genuine Gothic features; and other parts with circular arches, and the ornaments in the mixed and unsettled style of the early "revival."

The calendar, especially, exhibits a very singular blending of the two styles, which are so very uncongenial in character; but yet, the general effect produced is rich and agreeable.

Our specimen from this volume contains a portion of an office of the Catholic Church, and at the top, on the gold ground, a sort of summary, or explanation of the office, in French; all the offices, and some of the principal pictures, have explanations of this sort at the top or bottom of the page, and generally on a gold ground, or in writing of another colour, to distinguish them from the rest of the text.

sancta trinitas. R Sit no
men domini benedictum.
Ps. Exbc nunc z usqzi
seculum. Oremus Oratio.
Protector in te spe
rancium deus
sine quo nichil est uali
dum nichil sanctum mul
tiplica super nos misericor
diam tuam: Vt te rectore
te duce sic transeamus p
bona temporalia ut non
amittamus eterna. Per
xpm dominum. S. lucam

A BEAUTIFUL MANUSCRIPT IN CAMEÉ-GRIS, CONTAINING DIALOGUES OF FRANCIS I. OF FRANCE, AND JULIUS CÆSAR.

PRESERVED IN THE BRITISH MUSEUM.

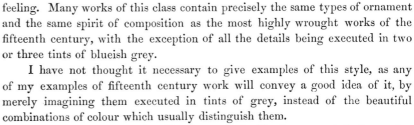

Francoys par la grace de Dieu Roy de France, second Cæsar, victeur & domateur des Souyces le dernier iour D'Avril, cinq mois apres la nativité de son second fils en son parc de Sainct Germain en Laye recontra Jule Cæsar & l'interroga fubtilement du contenu son premier lyure des commentaires.

Cæsar, premier subiugateur des belueces luy fyt gracieufe refponse en l'aduertiffant veritablement de la nature des Souyces & Allemans & de plufieurs aultres choses bonnes & profitables defquels on le doyt croyre, car il eft seur & fiable lefmoing, non parlant par ouyr dire.

AT the close of the fifteenth century, when gorgeousness of colour and intricacy of design had done their utmost in the art of illumination, novelty of effect was sought by means of simplicity of form and sobriety of colour. The books decorated in cameé-gris, or grisaille as it has been called, are examples of this feeling. Many works of this class contain precisely the same types of ornament and the same spirit of composition as the most highly wrought works of the fifteenth century, with the exception of all the details being executed in two or three tints of blueish grey.

I have not thought it necessary to give examples of this style, as any of my examples of fifteenth century work will convey a good idea of it, by merely imagining them executed in tints of grey, instead of the beautiful combinations of colour which usually distinguish them.

Another class of artist illuminators of this latter period, bestowing infinitely less labour upon the decorative borders, and concentrating their energies upon the miniatures, wrought out a style which, though less decorative, contains suggestive features which, even in a decorative point of view, may be highly valuable.

The beautiful book from which our two specimens are taken is a fine example of this last-mentioned school. In the first page, though the arabesqued border of former periods has been altogether abandoned and the margin left quite plain, yet a chaste decorative effect has been obtained by the introduction of the medallion portraits of Francis and Cæsar, carefully painted to imitate white relief, on a rich blue ground—an effect similar to that of the celebrated Portland vase; and possibly the artist had seen antique glass cameos of that description which suggested the idea, for that he was aware of the aids to be obtained from the remains of antiquity is proved by the head of Cæsar, which is evidently copied from a Roman coin.

The tablets forming the border to this description are the first page of the manuscript, and exhibit an ingenious arrangement, by which a frontispiece, a title, and, in fact, a preface to the book, are combined in one feature.

The book contains a great number of highly wrought miniatures, similar in general character to our second specimen, but infinitely varied in the treatment of detail and effect. There are sieges, attacks in mountain passes, march scenes, camp scenes, &c., in endless variety; but some of the night scenes are perhaps the most beautiful, in which the effect of fires, and also of the stars, produced by means of gold, is very beautiful and ingenious; and the careful and graceful drawing of the figures in that feeling of almost overwrought elegance which belongs to the period of the *renaissance*, stands quite unrivalled by any manuscript of the class that I have seen, except one in the Arsenal of Paris, containing the triumphs of Petrarch, by the same hand, the same signature, G., being found on the little tablets, and on one of them, first noticed by Dr. Waagen, the name at full, Godefroy. He appears to have been a great master of his art, and the French school of the "Renaissance," the school of Fontainbleau, as it is sometimes termed, has scarcely a more elegant representative.

Although Godefroy appears, as I have said, to have been acquainted with the beautiful remains of ancient art, yet in these miniatures, though relating to the times of Julius Cæsar, many of the costumes are of the period of Francis I.; but even in this anachronism the artist has preserved a sort of consistency, for Cæsar and his legions generally appear in a dress of a more Romanised character, while he appears to have satisfied himself that the costume of the Gallic tribes was the same fifty years before the Christian era as in the year 1519, at which time, according to a date affixed to most of the miniatures, he appears to have executed his work.

The principal object of the present work is to trace the progress and development of decorative art as exhibited in illuminated books; it has, consequently, more to do with the strictly ornamental portions, than with the miniatures, which belong more particularly to a history of painting. Therefore, such miniatures as I have selected for examples in this work, have presented decorative features also, as is the case in the present instance, where I may especially point out the judicious use of colour, as blue, red, and gold, in addition to the grey; which by their happy employment enrich and enliven the heaviness of that sober tone, without destroying the unity of effect, or producing the slightest patchiness, as will be readily acknowledged on reference to our example, representing a meeting between Ariovistus, a Gallic chief, and Cæsar. There are no enriched capitals in the volumes, the text being only varied by the occasional introduction of blue or gold letters of the ordinary forms. There is a curious map of France at the commencement of the volume.

feruiroit feulement de garde, ou
coborte pretoriaine.& ıe les faifois
bômeʒ darmeʒ & les mettoys tous
a cheual

Addition:

Legion eft affeʒ decleree parcida
uant Auffi eft coborte pretoriane

Le Roy demande

En quelle forte eftieʒ vous quãt võs
parlafleʒ a Ariouiftus

Le tref creftian Roy
Francoys

Demande a Cæfar

EN quanteʒ partieʒ eft diui
fee toute la gaule qui uous
a aultrefforʒ tant donne depeine
Cæfar dicteʒ le moy ıe vous prie

Cæfar respond

Roy liberal & pacifique vray
heritier de ma gloire et fortu

THE VENETIAN DIPLOMA OF SEMITECOLO.

 F illuminated books, very interesting specimens are to be found among the small volumes containing the diplomas or appointments issued by the Venetian State, to the governors of its towns and dependencies. These books are termed *ducali*, from the ducal title of the chief of the Venetian republic, and generally contain at least one richly illuminated page at the commencement, serving as a title or frontispiece. Sometimes these illuminated pictures apparently represent the new governor receiving his appointment; and at other times, as it would appear, taking his oath of fidelity to the government, before his patron saint. Others, again, appear to represent the Venetian Treasury, an apartment opening to the Adriatic, and surrounded with ships of all nations pouring in their tributary wealth: whilst some have merely a frontispiece of ornamental arabesque, but, most generally, they contain the portrait of the person receiving the appointment as some have fancifully supposed, to serve as a guarantee to distant dependencies that he was *de facto* the true governor appointed, as proved by his pictorial description appended to the diploma, like the written personal description attached to a modern Continental passport; a simile, however, somewhat incorrect, as the Venetian government was too strict to adopt any form that would admit of the slightest doubt.

In the instance of the specimen we have selected from the fine collection of these documents in the British Museum, on account of the beautiful miniature painting of the illumination, the new governor is apparently represented, in an attitude of prayer before the Virgin Mary in front of the figure of his patron saint, whose hand exhibits the stigmata described in the well known legend.

The diploma to which this miniature is attached bears the date 1644, and is from the Doge Francesco Molino, appointing Giovanni Semitecolo a noble Venetian, Conte, or Governor, of Pago and Isola, on the coast of Dalmatia. The governor of these possessions, it appears, was styled a Conte, but almost every Venetian dependence gave a different title to its temporary chief; some bearing the title of Podestà, some of Provveditore, Rettore, &c. &c., variously applied, according to usage, and the importance of the place. The present document is commenced in the ordinary form as follows :—

NOS
FRANCISCVS
MOLINO
DEI GRA DVX
VENETIAR.

in Roman capitals, disposed exactly as printed; but in the original, they are gilt. It then continues in a simple, running, and very modern-looking hand, evidently the work of an under-secretary or clerk; the first phrase commencing being the usual "Committimus tibi nobili viro Johanni Semitecolo," &c. &c.

From this it would seem quite clear that we may expect to find in the illumination the portrait of Giovanni Semitecolo; for the kneeling figure is evidently not the Doge Molino, as he does not wear the usual horned bonnet of the ducal chiefs of Venice. It thus appears quite clear, that it must be Semitecolo making his vows upon his appointment. We are not, however, to be so easily satisfied; and an examination of the arms emblazoned in the gilded framework of the illumination appears to prove that the portrait is neither that of Semitecolo nor Molino; for the arms in question are those of Priuli, a noble Venetian family, whose members have, at different times, filled most of the high offices of the state, not excepting the supreme one of Doge. It is also to be remarked, that the saint is not St. Giovanni, the patron of Semitecolo, but St. Francis.

From these circumstances, the inference would appear to be, that the miniature was not originally painted for the present diploma, but has belonged to some other, appointing a member of the Priuli family to a similar office. The extreme beauty of the painting, also, would induce us to assign the miniature not only to another diploma, but to one of an earlier date; the graceful and masterly drawing, and grandeur of style evincing a higher phasis of art than existed at that period; and both the dress and cut of the beard of the kneeling figure would induce us to assign it to a considerably earlier date, and possibly to the hand of one of the great Italian masters: as the greatest of them, if appointed to the office of painter to the Venetian State, was employed to ornament important diplomas of this description; and even Titian himself is said to have adorned several with his inimitable works. With respect to the style of the beard, most of our readers will recollect that in 1644, the period of our Charles I., the small pointed beard was general all over Europe, while the flowing beard, such as represented in this portrait, had completely disappeared nearly half a century before. Much stress, however, cannot be laid on the style of dress, as it appears to be, not a private costume, but the state robe of a Venetian senator. The mystery of the connexion of the miniature with the diploma may possibly be explained, by supposing that when many of these documents were scattered at the time of the invasion of Venice by the French revolutionists, some person having obtained possession of several, supplied the defect of a damaged miniature in the present book, from some other of the same description which he might be induced to do on account of the very perfect state of the binding of the Semitecolo diploma, which is undoubtedly the original one, having the winged and crowned Lion of St. Mark on one side, and the usual motto " Pax tibi Marce Evangelista meus" on the other; and so, perhaps, a still more interesting document may have been destroyed, to render this one apparently perfect. It appears, finally, quite evident, that this frontispiece, though certainly belonging to a Venetian ducale, does not belong to the one in question. The arms used as an O, at the commencement of this description, are those of Semitecolo, obtained from another source.

COMMENTARIES ON ST. PAUL'S EPISTLE TO THE ROMANS,

ILLUMINATED BY GUILIO CLOVIO, IN THE SOANE MUSEUM.

IN Italy, the art of illumination had been carried to the highest pitch of artistic excellence by Francesco, and Girolamo dai Libri; of this excellence the celebrated volume of "Hours," executed for the Duchess of Urbino, and now in the Bodleian Library of Oxford, is a most exquisite example. It is rich in the extreme, both in detail and in finish, and yet the drawing and composition of some of the miniatures with which it is most profusely decorated, are almost worthy of the pencil of Raphael himself, in purity of design and beautiful sentiment of expression. These illuminators were succeeded, in the glories of their art, by Guilio Grovata, more generally known as Guilio Clovio, a pupil of Raphael's greatest scholar, Guilio Romano. Clovio was born in 1498, and died in 1578, he did not surpass Girolamo dai Libri, whose pupil he had also been, either in finish or composition, and was inferior to him in that chasteness and sobriety of combination, both of form and colour, that distinguishes the works of that period. But his glittering and gorgeous combinations of tone, combined with a more florid style, impart an air of splendour to his illuminations which has never been approached by any other illuminator. His most celebrated work is that in the private library of the kings of Naples, preserved in a gold cover, profusely enriched with gems of great value. But even a sight of this magnificent book is a privilege obtained by few. The well-known manuscript Dante, of the Vatican Library, is another glittering work of the pencil of Clovio. These, with the works formerly preserved in the chapel of the Farnesi Palace at Rome, with one or two others, are the monuments upon which the fame of Clovio now rests; and the rarity of his works adds not a little to their value. His fame was greater than in the present degraded state of decorative art we can conceive, for a fine medal was struck to his memory, which is preserved in the College of Brera, at Milan.

The present examples may be said to be from the only work of this illuminator which has found its way to England; for the illuminated "Hours," said to be from the pencil of Clovio, which were formerly at Strawberry Hill, are certainly not the fruit of his own pencil, although they may be of his school. While the illuminations I have selected, as an example of this great artist, bear, in addition to other undoubted evidences of style, &c., the artist's own signature, in a corner of the border of the frontispiece, which may be literally translated:—"For Marino Grimani, Cardinal and Legate of Perugia, his patron, painted by Guilio Grovata;" his surname of *Clovio* seldom being found attached to his works. The volume from which they are taken forms the chief ornament of the library of the Soane Museum, and consists of Commentaries on the Epistles of Paul to the Romans. It was purchased, with two smaller manuscripts, of the late Duke of Buckingham, for the sum of one thousand guineas.

The frontispiece and first page exhibited in the annexed plates form, with the border of this description, and a few capital letters, the only ornaments of the volume, but their elaborate character compensates for a number of less highly wrought decorations. Indeed, at this period, and even previously, it became customary only to ornament the first two pages of works, and sometimes only a single first page, for the more artistic quality of the ornaments rendered the former profusion impossible, except in very rare cases. For the value of labour had greatly increased, and illuminated books were no longer the sole production of the *scriptorium* of the convent, but frequently the work of artists who had to realize an income from the exercise of the art as a profession. The skilful manner in which the borderings of the frontispiece are composed is worthy of examination by every student of decorative art. The different objects are not placed one above another without any apparent means of support, but are sustained by finely-drawn Michaelangiolesque figures, which might almost be compared to those that sustain the massive painted architecture of the ceiling of the Sistine Chapel. Thus suspended, appear medallions, trophies, and other objects, wrought with almost miraculous skill, of which no mechanical production, however perfect, can convey an idea. The medallions sometimes contain relievos in gold, and sometimes highly-coloured miniatures, of most elaborate execution. That of the "Stoning of St. Stephen," supported by a group of infant figures, and surrounded by trophies of war, and emblems of peace, is very beautiful; and the female figure apparently personifying Peace extinguishing the torch of war, is wrought with such exquisite care, that it may be compared to the most highly-finished painting on ivory. The figure of Mars, or an emblematic male figure personifying War, occupies a corresponding position on the opposite page, and balances the effect of the female figure in the border of the frontispiece. The principal feature of which latter is the large miniature, occupying the entire space within the borders, representing the "Conversion of St. Paul." The peculiarities of its treatment afford a good example both of the excellencies and defects of Guilio Clovio as an artist in the higher walks of his profession, and strengthen the supposition that the fine series of drawings bequeathed by the late Mr. Grenville to the British Museum, being coloured copies of a well-known series of early engravings, said to have been executed by Guilio Clovio for the Emperor Charles V., may really be the work of our illuminator, for the style of finish and tone of colouring both strongly resemble this large and elaborate miniature of the "Conversion of St. Paul."

The second page of our specimen may be said to contain the commencement of the work. Its general character of decoration is similar to that of the opposite page—indeed, purposely made to correspond, as I have stated in alluding to the figure of Mars, or War; but the portrait of the Cardinal Grimani, in the exterior border, and the arms supported by most gorgeously-coloured dragons in the lower border, are worthy of especial examination.

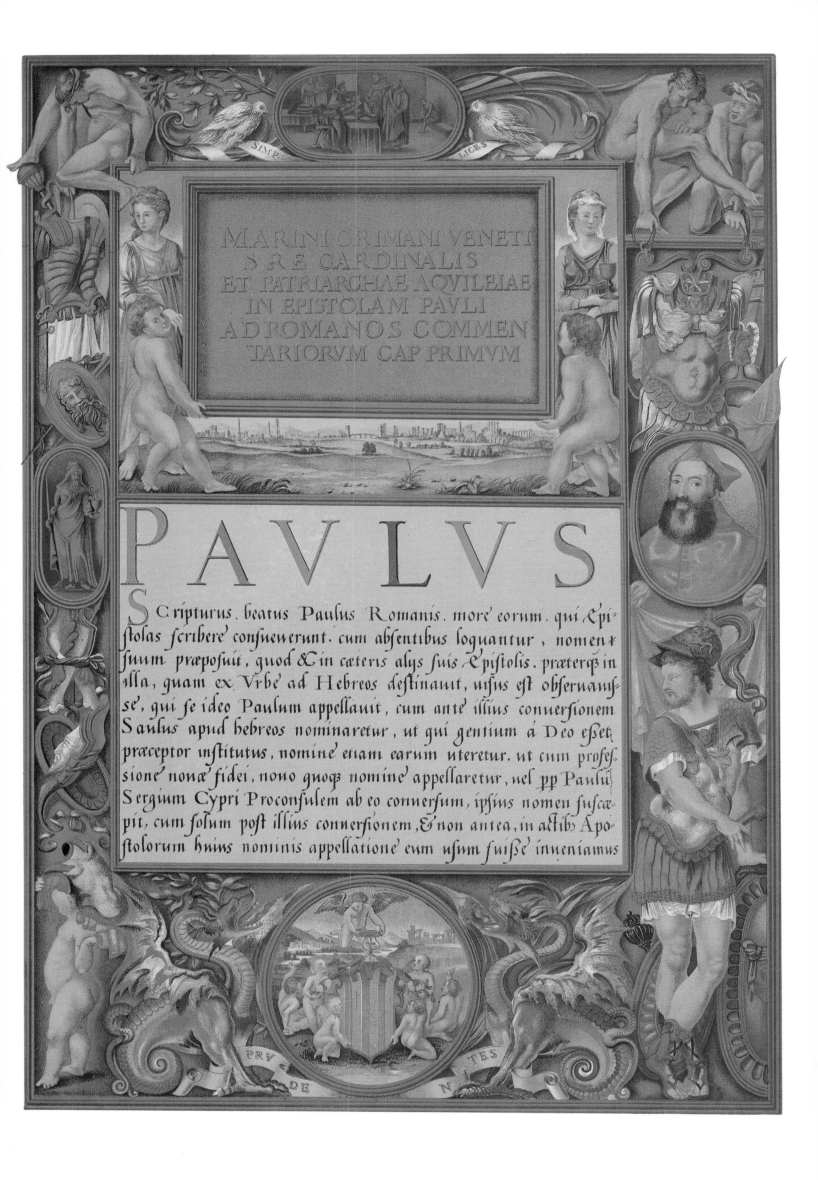

MARINI GRIMANI VENETI
S R E CARDINALIS
ET PATRIARCHAE AQVILEIAE
IN EPISTOLAM PAVLI
AD ROMANOS COMMEN
TARIORVM CAP PRIMVM

PAVLVS

Scripturus. beatus Paulus Romanis. more eorum. qui Epi-
stolas scribere consueuerunt. cum absentibus loquantur, nomen
suum praeposuit, quod & in caeteris alys suis Epistolis. praeterq in
illa, quam ex Vrbe ad Hebreos destinauit, usus est obseruauis-
se, qui se ideo Paulum appellauit, cum ante illius conuersionem
Saulus apud hebreos nominaretur, ut qui gentium á Deo esset
praeceptor institutus, nomine etiam earum uteretur. ut cum profes-
sione nouae fidei, nouo quoqz nomine appellaretur, uel pp Paulũ
Sergium Cypri Proconsulem ab eo conuersum, ipsius nomen suscae-
pit, cum solum post illius conuersionem, & non antea, in actibz Apo-
stolorum huius nominis appellatione eum usum fuisse inueniamus

THE PRAYER-BOOK OF LOUIS XIV.

IN THE BIBLIOTHEQUE DU ROI, PARIS.

THIS manuscript is one of the latest specimens of the true illuminated missal. The style is that of the decorative art of the middle of the seventeenth century, as worked out (more especially by Le Brun and Le Pautre) in the palace and gardens of Versailles, and known in French artistic nomenclature as " *le genre Versailles.*"

This book, though the prayer-book of the King himself, is not equal in the style of art and brilliancy of treatment to other manuscripts of the same period—the great book, for instance, shown to continental travellers, in the public library of Rouen ; or the prayer-book of " Madame de la Valliere," as it is termed, at present in a private collection in this country ; but, as presenting more *variety* in the ornaments and composition, it was deemed a better general example of the style of the period—particularly as the extent of our work precludes the possibility of giving more than one.

Miniatures, executed entirely in one brilliant colour, such as green, red, or blue, heightened with gold, form the most attractive feature of illuminated books of this period ; and these, it will be seen, are very successfully treated in our specimen, whilst some pages of the same manuscript (less suitable to our purpose in other respects) exhibit miniature pictures of this description, possessing a very high order of merit as artistic compositions.

Our specimen page contains a portion of the Roman Catholic Church service. The capitals, it will be observed, are much in the style of late Italian manuscripts.

The general composition of the ornaments of the page, though not possessing the same completeness, continuity, and appropriateness of design as is found in earlier periods of the art of illumination, yet forms a rich ensemble, very far from unpleasing to the eye.

Susanné   accusée

Sit & benedictio:
Procedenti ab utroque.
Compar sit laudatio. Amen.
Verf. Panem de cælo præstitisti eis, alleluia.
Resp. Omne delectamentum in se habentem,
alleluia.
Ad Magnificat Antiphona.
Sacrum convivium, in quo Chri =
stus sumitur recolitur memoria.
passionis ejus, mens impletur gra-
tiâ, & futuræ gloriæ nobis pignus
datur, alleliua.
Canticum B Mariæ Virginis.
Agnificat: anima mea Dnũm.
Et exultavit spiritus meus: in
Deo salutari meo.
Quia respexit humilitatem
ancillæ suæ: ecce enim ex hoc beatam
me dicent omnes generationes.

120.